So You Want to Work in Crypto

Not Law, Not Medicine, But Crypto

Alexander Rees-Evans

So You Want to Work in Crypto: Not Law, Not Medicine, But Crypto

Alexander Rees-Evans
Allauch, France

ISBN-13 (pbk): 979-8-8688-0502-8
https://doi.org/10.1007/979-8-8688-0503-5

ISBN-13 (electronic): 979-8-8688-0503-5

Managing Director, Apress Media LLC: Welmoed Spahr
Acquisitions Editor: Malini Rajendran
Development Editor: James Markham
Editorial Project Manager: Gryffin Winkler

Cover Photo by Art Rachen on Unsplash

Distributed to the book trade worldwide by Springer Science+Business Media New York, 1 New York Plaza, Suite 4600, New York, NY 10004-1562, USA. Phone 1-800-SPRINGER, fax (201) 348-4505, e-mail orders-ny@springer-sbm.com, or visit www.springeronline.com. Apress Media, LLC is a California LLC and the sole member (owner) is Springer Science + Business Media Finance Inc (SSBM Finance Inc). SSBM Finance Inc is a **Delaware** corporation.

For information on translations, please e-mail booktranslations@springernature.com; for reprint, paperback, or audio rights, please e-mail bookpermissions@springernature.com.

Apress titles may be purchased in bulk for academic, corporate, or promotional use. eBook versions and licenses are also available for most titles. For more information, reference our Print and eBook Bulk Sales web page at http://www.apress.com/bulk-sales.

Any source code or other supplementary material referenced by the author in this book is available to readers on GitHub. For more detailed information, please visit https://www.apress.com/gp/services/source-code.

If disposing of this product, please recycle the paper

To my beloved partner Manon and son Sandro.

Table of Contents

About the Author

 **Alexander T. Rees-Evans** is a veteran in the world of crypto, initially collaborating with the luxury asset trading platform, Idoneus. One of his first successes was convincing the French royal family to accept crypto as a method of payment for their Champagne "Heritage." Since then, he has headed up large sales teams in a centralized exchange, private placement platforms and was the international sales director at Kaizen Finance, where over 40 projects were built and launched.

Rees-Evans is currently a senior advisor at DVerse, a multi-award-winning Web3 consultancy firm working with some of the largest companies in this space such as Algorand, Farcana, Animoca Brands, and Assassin's Creed. He also presides over the blockchain and cybernetic commission of the World Business Union, is a mentor at Techstars, Blockstart, Avio, and GeniusX, and an accredited partner of BTC Safezone, the most secure platform for exchanging Bitcoin and USDT.

About the Technical Reviewer

Leo (Leonardus) Woest is a seasoned professional with a dynamic career in the recruitment industry. A graduate of the University of Potchefstroom in South Africa, Leo relocated to the UK, where he built a successful career in recruitment. Leveraging his extensive experience, Leo transitioned to an in-house role with a leading cryptocurrency exchange and NFT marketplace. Known for his strategic approach and deep understanding of the recruitment and HR sectors, Leo is dedicated to fostering growth and innovation within the industry.

Acknowledgments

A special thank you to the European Blockchain Association, World Business Union, and the Dubai Blockchain Center.

Introduction

In this book, you will find not only an introduction to Web3, but you will embark on a deep and detailed journey of the corporate side of this industry. At the beginning, you will start to learn about the actual working environment of Web3 and explore what it is like to operate full-time in this revolutionary environment. Secondly, we will focus on the key differences between working in the traditional world in contrast to this high-paced merging sector so you don't get left behind. Moving on, we will delve into all of the various jobs that this industry has to offer, most of which you may not have expected. Adding to this, we will learn which jobs are most suited to your background so you can have a seamless onboarding for your first crypto job. Another major component of this industry that affects jobs heavily is the cycles and market sentiments; these intricacies will be explained in great detail too. One of the more unique aspects of companies in this industry is their fiscal domiciles and contracts; if not understood properly, you may miss a good opportunity, so a whole chapter is dedicated to examining them. The general company cultures and working environments are next on the list too; you'll fully comprehend what it's like to actually work in this industry full time. Next on the list, we'll learn what you need to bulk up on and how to prepare for your crypto interview, ensuring you the best possible chances to get that dream job. Leaving no rock unturned, we'll be exploring the entire onboarding process, including tests, general industry knowledge, and how to successfully be part of the team. What's more is that we'll also be looking into your first day at work, what's expected of you, the different tools you'll be expected to use, and even how to ace your very first day. Nearing the end of the book, you will discover how to keep your job in crypto without falling behind, noting all of the metrics and efforts you'll be expected to make. In the ending pages of this book, you'll finally absorb industry insights, strategy, tips, and hacks on how to positively evolve your career in this wonderful industry, making sure that you don't just get a job, but you have a stellar career!

CHAPTER 1

Introduction to Working in Crypto

Welcome to the world of crypto – a realm where traditional work norms are constantly redefined and the future of finance and technology intertwine in exciting and unexpected ways. This book is your gateway to understanding the opportunities, challenges, tips, tricks, and hacks for developing your career within the rewarding cryptocurrency industry. This space can be one of the most challenging yet equally rewarding spaces to work in due to its unique attributes and general culture. In order to enter, succeed, and thrive in the wonderful world of crypto, you will need to prepare yourself, as this industry differs heavily from any other in existence today. You may also be wondering what you need to bulk up on, what jobs exist, and just what is it really like to work in this revolutionary space overflowing with mystery. In the first chapter of this book, we will explore just that! Prior to obtaining your first job in crypto, you need to understand what it's actually like working full-time in this industry in contrast with all of the stigma, speculation, and confusion cast upon it by the legacy media and institutions.

Cryptocurrencies and digital assets are no longer simply speculative scams involving a few geeks and degens. Major corporations such as BlackRock, Fidelity, top-tier established banks, and even governments are getting involved now. This new wave of institutional adoption not only opens huge new lines of funding and future jobs but also

© Alexander Rees-Evans 2024
A. Rees-Evans, *So You Want to Work in Crypto*,
https://doi.org/10.1007/979-8-8688-0503-5_1

the much-needed validation this industry deserves. Moreover, the seriousness of the players getting involved can only help but encourage more individuals like yourself to take that life-changing decision of working full-time in this revolutionary and meaningful sector.

To get the ball rolling, the first chapter of this book will provide you with real industry insight on just what it's like to work in crypto, ensuring you a unique and realistic perspective of the crypto world!

Ecosystem and Environment

Now the cryptocurrency industry, often symbolized by the groundbreaking emergence of Bitcoin, has evolved into a sprawling ecosystem encompassing not just digital currencies but an array of innovative technologies and applications. This new era in finance and tech has given birth to a work culture that is as dynamic and multifaceted as the technologies it champions. As crypto is inherently global, it knows no borders. This digital frontier is home to a decentralized ethos where traditional corporate hierarchies dissolve into more fluid and dynamic structures. In this world, your colleagues might be spread across the globe, each contributing from different cultures, time zones, and perspectives. This global melting pot is a breeding ground for innovative ideas and approaches, making working in crypto a continuously enriching experience. This industry also operates on a non-stop cycle. The global nature of the market means that it never sleeps, and for those working within it, this can mean adapting to an unconventional and flexible work schedule. Here, responsiveness and adaptability are key, as the market's pulse can quicken at a moment's notice, often requiring immediate attention and action.

Inclusiveness

One of the most compelling aspects of the crypto industry is its inclusive approach to skills and backgrounds. Whether you're a seasoned developer, a finance professional, a creative marketer, or a curious newcomer, there's a place for you in crypto. This industry values skill diversity and continuous learning, with a keen emphasis on staying abreast of rapidly evolving technologies and market trends. At its core, the crypto sector is driven by a spirit of innovation and disruption. Working in this space means being part of an environment that is constantly pushing the boundaries of what's possible, be it through the development of new blockchain technologies, exploration of decentralized finance (DeFi), or the creation of groundbreaking digital assets like NFTs (Non-Fungible Tokens) or Ordinals. Another interesting aspect is remote work. It's the backbone of the crypto industry, offering flexibility and the freedom to work from anywhere. This comes with its own set of challenges, from managing time zones to maintaining work-life balance. Successfully navigating this aspect of crypto work requires discipline, excellent communication skills, and the hunger of striving for greatness. In Web3, collaboration is key. The decentralized nature of the industry fosters a culture where teamwork and collective problem-solving are highly valued.

Meritocracy

Meritocracy rules in this realm; what counts most is the value you bring to the table. This emphasis on merit and contribution creates an environment where creativity and performance are recognized and rewarded. However, with high rewards come high risks. The market is known for its volatility, and working in this space can sometimes feel like riding a rollercoaster. This requires a certain level of resilience and a mindset that embraces both the highs and the lows as part of the journey. For those with a passion for the industry, these fluctuations often add to the excitement and challenge

3

of the work. Every person with a slightly entrepreneurial mindset or an ounce of ambition will definitely find themselves at home in Web3. Working in the crypto industry is more than just a job; it's an adventure into the future of technology and finance. It's a path that promises continuous learning, growth, and the opportunity to be at the forefront of a digital revolution. As we delve deeper into the specifics of this unique work environment in the following sections, you'll gain insights into the nuances of the traditional corporate environment to the Web3 environment, the exhilarating experience of travelling the world and creating huge value through disruption. Furthermore, the opportunities, salaries, and evolution perspectives of the industry, all of the tips, tricks, and hacks to be successfully onboarded, plus the distinct vibe and expectations that characterize employee interactions in crypto will be deconstructed and analyzed in detail. Dear reader, this is more than just a career path; this is a life-changing journey into the heart of innovation, and your journey starts here.

Working in the Crypto World

To kick things off, let's explore a little more on what it's actually like to work in crypto. In this exhilarating world, even the concept of an office is redefined. Forget the four walls and a water cooler; your workspace spans continents and time zones. Here, in the crypto cosmos, you're as likely to collaborate with partners from Singapore as you are to brainstorm with a blockchain expert in Berlin, all from the comfort of your home or a local café. Now it's not because you can work from Starbucks while showing off your pumpkin spice latte and new Macbook Pro to passersby that you do it all of the time. The goal is to still work in a relatively professional environment, noting that on top of this, you often have video conferences where you need to speak clearly. Plus, I'm pretty sure the other hipsters in Starbucks won't appreciate hearing you speak about the internal company action plans for 50 minutes or so…

A Dance in Space and Time

Working in crypto is a dance with space and time. The market never sleeps, and neither does the buzz of activity. You find yourself adapting to the rhythms of a 24/7 work cycle, where late-night strategy sessions and early morning updates become part of your routine. When you really don't have an option, sure, you can take a few calls from a café, but just don't let it become the norm. This round-the-clock operation means staying flexible and ever-ready, but it also demands a mastery of work-life balance. It's about knowing when to power through and when to power down, ensuring that while you're riding the crypto wave, you don't burn out. Working in crypto is a marathon, not a sprint. Additionally, one of the trickiest aspects of this global workplace is navigating the maze of time zones. Scheduling a meeting? You might need to juggle between EST, GMT, and IST. The key lies in clever planning and staying organized. Tools like time zone converters and Calendly become your best friends, helping you stay connected and in sync with your global team and clients. It's about finding that sweet spot where your work hours overlap with your colleagues halfway across the world. Often, you do have to sacrifice sleep depending on what country you live in and which time zone the company you work for operates within.

Communication Platforms

On top of staying on top of this, you'll need to master a lot of platforms like Slack, Zoom, ClickUp, and CRMs, which we'll dive into in Chapter 9 of this book. These are the new office spaces, where ideas are exchanged, and projects come to life. These digital tools break down geographical barriers, enabling seamless collaboration. But they're more than just utilities; they're the virtual water coolers, the spaces where you connect, share a laugh, and build team spirit, despite the physical distance. One of the most enriching aspects of working in a global environment is the exposure to different cultures. Each interaction is an opportunity to learn and grow to understand perspectives vastly different from your own. This diversity is not just a source of learning; it's a wellspring of creativity. It challenges you to think broader, to approach problems from angles you hadn't considered, and to find solutions that are as diverse as the team crafting them. The 24/7 international remote environment of the crypto world is a dynamic and challenging arena. It's an environment that demands adaptability, embraces diversity, and rewards innovation. It's where work is not confined by geography, but rather where each day is different, and where the possibilities are as limitless as the technology driving it. For those who thrive in a fast-paced, ever-changing landscape, this will become your new playground.

Conferences

Wait, how can someone write a book on working in crypto if we don't speak about the conferences? These are the places where it all started, aren't they?

They are indeed, back in the early days when Bitcoin was frowned upon as a bad joke, the real OGs would organize get-togethers in bars and restaurants with other early adopters and just speak about Bitcoin. As time went on, these gatherings became larger and larger by their attendance and their contents. As blockchain technologies developed and altcoins emerged, crypto conferences soon became the very epicenters of this international growth. Since the early days, they have become an even more important part of the ecosystem, bringing hundreds of thousands of people together all over the world every year. Global conferences are not just events; they are grand odysseys that take you to the heart of the action. These gatherings are where the pulse of the industry beats the strongest. From the glamorous high-rises of Dubai to the historical elegance of European capitals, crypto conferences are a non-negotiable step of working in Web3.

As you've understood, these conferences are more than business meetups; they're melting pots of culture, innovation, and networking. Imagine mingling with the brightest minds in blockchain against the backdrop of an ancient city or discussing the future of finance under the stars on a beach. It's here, amid these diverse settings, that you form connections that go beyond mere professional networks. They become cultural exchanges, learning experiences, and sometimes the start of lifelong friendships. But travelling the world for crypto conferences isn't just about boarding flights and shaking hands. It's a strategic endeavor. Choosing which conferences to attend can be as crucial as the deals you strike there. It's about aligning your travel with your professional goals, be it learning, networking, or business development. Of course, if you're hired into a well-funded company, often the expenses and planning are usually taken care of. It's, however, important to note that even if the company takes care of travel and hotel expenses, you may have to pay them upfront and be reimbursed afterwards. Even taking care of your Uber fares going to and from the conference and various side events isn't uncommon. Remember, you're in the startup world of which the biggest companies have been around for ten years tops! Consider yourself lucky to be in the position and place you are in; moreover, make the most of it not just for the company you'll be working for but for yourself. As conferences don't really last more than a few days, it's all about maximizing every moment. Attend the keynotes, join the breakout sessions, and be part of the after-parties. But more importantly, be present. Engage in conversations with random people, ask questions, and really put yourself out there!

Side Events

Another major, non-negotiable part of crypto conferences is the side event club. For every main conference, there's anywhere from twenty to a few hundred side events. Each and every one of them is organized by private entities such as blockchains, Web3 labs, crypto projects, market makers, Know Your Customer (KYC - Glossary n°6) providers, exchanges, and more. Literally every big brand hosts and tries to throw the one! You have chilled versions during the day, where you may find yourself sipping champagne while listening to a pitch in a penthouse overlooking the sea in Miami. To crazy afterparties once the sun sets, ending up on the dancefloor of a privatized nightclub or bar drinking rum and coke while trying to speak with a tipsy investor from Singapore. Crypto side events really are the best places to be during conferences, but as they're private, you need to reserve in advance. What exactly do you need to reserve, and how on earth do you know what side events are on? These are some of the things you will wonder when attending your first conferences. The answers are pretty straightforward; you need to know people. Of course, when you're starting off, it's virtually impossible to access them this way. Your best bet would purely be to mingle with as many people at the main conference as possible, and when appropriate, simply ask what side events they'll be heading to after. This way, you can ask them to send you the digital registration forms for the side events they're attending. If you do this with ten people, you should have a pretty vast list, choice, and access to the majority of the most influential side events available. All that's left to do is register yourself to the ones of interest, bearing in mind some may be pretty far away, so do take travel formalities into consideration prior to engaging.

After your first full-on conference, you'll understand what I mean when I say you get very very tired, very very fast. You basically mix three or four evenings of non-stop partying until six in the morning with walking a few kilometers per day in a suit and tailored shoes, then back to the conference everyday mingling and eating finger food combined with heavy jet lag. If you're lucky enough, in some rare moments of downtime, do try to soak in the local culture, the food, the art, just the general rhythm of the city you're in. These experiences not only enrich you personally but also provide a broader perspective on the type of business you can get done over there. The impact of these global conferences on your professional and personal life can really be profound. They're platforms for learning about the latest trends, hooking up with crypto celebs, and getting a sense of where the industry is heading. The connections made here can lead to collaborations, investments, and sometimes, a whole new direction in your career. They're catalysts for growth, both for individuals and for businesses.

A Lifestyle

The crypto industry is not just a workplace; it's a lifestyle. Forget the 9-to-5 and having carefree weekends. Crypto is "Decentralized Finance" so a lot like Wall Street, it never sleeps. If you really want to be successful in Web3, you have to be willing to accept the culture, a community driven by passion and the pursuit of non-stop innovation. It's a world where the conventional corporate vibe is replaced by a dynamic, start-up spirit. Here, hierarchies are flattened, ideas reign supreme, and everyone, from interns to CEOs, is a part of the brainstorming process. In the decentralized world of crypto, building relationships is an art. With teams spread across the globe, often the only connection is a screen. But within this digital realm, bonds are forged over shared goals and late-night project sessions. The relationships here are built on mutual respect, a shared passion for crypto, and a commitment to pushing boundaries. Because all of your surrounding colleagues and fellow employees have the exact same hunger and drive as yourself, there's an unspoken bond that forms in crypto teams. It's a sense of being in this together, tackling challenges, celebrating victories, and sometimes, navigating losses. It's a bond that's strengthened by the unique nature of the work – the highs and lows of the market, the thrill of innovation, and the shared journey in uncharted territory. I do believe that this is one of the reasons why it attracts a lot of ambitious individuals, all striving to develop a career in Web3. This is one of the reasons why the crypto workforce grows 80% year on year! Such information is extremely positive for the whole crypto ecosystem because it shows a real path and future for serious jobs and careers.

Summary

The future of work in crypto promises to be as dynamic as the industry itself. As technology evolves and the industry matures, so too will the way teams collaborate and relate. But one thing is certain: the culture of innovation, the drive for excellence, and the spirit of collaboration that define the crypto world today will continue to shape its tomorrow. Will you be a part of it?

In the next chapter, you'll see how the corporate and crypto worlds compare, providing you a sharp contrast between both of these worlds!

CHAPTER 2

Corporate vs. Crypto and Start-up Environment

The corporate and crypto worlds can be seen as two different planets in the same financial universe. One represents a legacy of structured business practices; the other, the frontier of financial technology. In this chapter, we'll compare these two worlds, exploring how they differ in their approach to risk, their operational structures, their cultural ethos, and their impact on the global economy. As we embark on this exploratory journey, we aim to prepare you for the fantastic, innovative, sprightly, brisk, world of crypto, which is nothing like the stable, proud, and wise corporate world. Understanding the subtleties and differences between the two worlds will enable you to succeed in not just getting a job in crypto but also developing and building your career with order and panache!

As blockchain technology matures in the third decade since its moment of decentralized fame in 2008, it is now better understood and taken more seriously; the number of crypto job openings is also increasing. As you're thinking of venturing down this path, it is useful for you to explore the differences between the corporate and crypto working environments. As each has its unique ethos, dynamics, and paradigms, this presents a fascinating study in contrast and comparison. This chapter is

© Alexander Rees-Evans 2024
A. Rees-Evans, *So You Want to Work in Crypto*,
https://doi.org/10.1007/979-8-8688-0503-5_2

applicable to graduates planning to start their working lives in the crypto industry as well as to mid-to-senior-level corporate executives interested in transitioning to the crypto world. The differences, challenges, and inherent nature of both worlds will be described, providing you with extra insight into how the structured, time-honored corporate environment is juxtaposed against the dynamic, uncharted waters of the crypto universe.

Corporate World

Picture a well-orchestrated symphony – this metaphor aptly describes the corporate world. Here, each element, from the lowliest intern to the CEO, functions as part of a larger, well-oiled machine. The corporate landscape has an established hierarchy, boasting time-tested strategies and procedures that have evolved over centuries of business practices. It's a world where predictability and stability are prized, where risk is calculated and mitigated, and where success is measured in steady growth and shareholder value. In the corporate world, hierarchy is not just a structure; it is enshrined in the corporate ladder and the employee growth structure. Companies operate on well-defined levels of authority and responsibility, creating an environment where order and protocol are key to lubricating the company's timeless wheels and cogs. This structure ensures clarity in roles, responsibilities, and processes, ensuring the corporate world operates in an orderly manner. More often than not, corporations tend to approach risk with great caution as they are accountable to shareholders and stakeholders. Market research, competitor analysis, and risk assessments are integral to corporate strategy. The focus is on sustainable growth, making the corporate world synonymous with stability. Corporates are masters of the long game. Strategies are developed not just for the next quarter but for years ahead! This foresight allows for long-term planning, resource allocation, and steady, machine-like progress toward defined goals.

Crypto World

Now, imagine a frontier town in Buffalo Bill's Wild West in the nineteenth century. This is the crypto world. It's a space of rapid innovation, dominated by high risks and rewards, where rules are being written and rewritten as the game unfolds – a stark contrast to the corporate environment. It's a realm where decentralization challenges traditional hierarchies, where market volatility is part of everyday life, and where the pace of change can be breathtakingly fast. The crypto world thrives on the principles of decentralization and immediate turnover. Away from traditional hierarchies, this fosters a culture of innovation and experimentation. It's an environment where new ideas are constantly explored and the status quo is regularly challenged. Even if volatility is the pulse of the crypto world, rest assured, this happens by cycles, some of which resemble those of traditional financial markets. We'll explore this in greater detail in Chapter 5: Market conditions and cycles. The prices of products and services in the Web 3 world do, however, possess a constant young flame with which prices can skyrocket or plummet within hours, making it a natural landscape of uncharted risks. High risks have always had the potential for high rewards, attracting those willing to navigate its turbulent waters. In the crypto world, change is the only constant. Technologies evolve rapidly, new tokens are launched daily, and regulatory landscapes are in flux. This constant state of change demands adaptability and agility, traits that define the crypto space and its inhabitants. In order to understand the differences between these two worlds, one must delve into the fabric of their existence, examining the risks that define and differentiate them at the core. This exploration is not just an academic exercise; it's a journey into the heart of what makes these wonderful sectors tick, their inherent contrasts, and how to adapt your risk management when transitioning into the crypto industry.

Risks in the Established Corporate World

Imagine yourself driving along your usual motorway, the weather, scenery, and tranquility of knowing when you must turn. No surprises. This is the predictable and unshakable corporate world. Here, risk is a closely calculated variable, often measured and mitigated through years of established practices and historical data accumulated over time. Corporate risk revolves around not just market competition but financial fluctuations and leverage points with some occasional operational challenges. Credit defaults, market risk, liquidity risk, operational risk, or even equity risk are just some of the exposures traditional corporations have to deal with. The playbook is hence well-defined and fine-tuned through market research, risk assessments, financial audits, and strategic long-term planning. In the corporate sphere, expansion is the game's name. Companies fight for market share, legacy reputation, and customer loyalty. However, all corporations face the risk of failing to innovate, stay relevant, and of being outmaneuvered by competitors in the long run. Nokia, the Finnish mobile phone company, and Kodak, the old camera company, are classic examples of legacy corporations whose principals weren't able to adapt and survive despite being market leaders. Jobs in the corporate sector have traditionally offered a safe and sure life-long career path. The traditional sector is obliged to not only promote constant long-term strategies but also try to navigate the turbulent waters of world-changing innovation to maintain their legacy status and stay on top. This said, large corporations do have deep pockets, big legal teams, years of experience and a very solid and well understood strategic framework. Here, risk management in finance involves diversifying investments, prudent financial planning, and often a very conservative approach to capital expenditure. A behemoth of a burly entity, slowly marching forward and hastening through the concrete walls of new markets while never looking back. As mighty and powerful they may be, it's important to note that they're also very slow to maneuver or make big strategic changes, sometimes leading to unexpected sudden bankruptcies, projecting ripple effects across all industries around the globe, like the financial crisis of 2008.

On the other side of the scale, legacy is replaced with ambition, long-term is replaced with immediate, and corporate is replaced with its much younger digital twin, crypto. Envision setting sail into the blue, open ocean, where the paper maps are being drawn in real-time and the world's brimming with adventure, welcome to the world of crypto. Here, risks are not just part of the game; they are the very essence of it. The crypto sector thrives on risk, yet has matured heavily since the early, more hectic juvenile days of emergence. Today, the risk is far more calculated and mitigated as hard lessons were learned from a lot of Web3 companies over the past years.

Lessons Learned

From Venture Capital (VC) funds to the average crypto start-up, due to poor decisions, low to near-nonexistent risk mitigation, and bad actors, billions of dollars have been ripped out of the ecosystem. The crypto industry is still heavily impacted by traditional financial industries well-being as crypto is at its core based in financial markets. This means that it's still affected by the same parameters as the traditional financial world, such as geopolitics, economics, wars, and the general market sentiment. Although it shares similar triggers, the endemic risks such as market manipulation, technology risk, price swings, and regulatory issues differ heavily from the traditional financial sector's. As we saw in 2022-2023, the Web3 industry relies on agile investors to inject capital into crypto projects; this is the oxygen of the industry. Without it, all crypto entities start to suffocate, leaving only those with enough runway to survive. Consider this as the industry hierarchy, investment firms are at the top; without them, everything grinds to a halt. Since then, a lot of investment firms filed for bankruptcy, leaving only the investment firms of which practiced serious risk mitigation as the remaining industry investors. Much like a double-edged sword, this did more good than bad to the sector, as every investment is now executed with greater caution and care, thanks to the remaining, mature investors. There are still some lucky mavericks known as the lead or angel investors, who pride themselves on being among the first to invest, but these do come with heightened risks – market volatility, project success, regulatory uncertainty, market competition, and security threats.

A True Paradox

Crypto markets have always been and will remain notorious for their high volatility, with prices capable of significant swings in short periods of time. This volatility offers a paradoxical situation, presenting both opportunities for high returns but also high risks for investors and projects alike. The lack of historical data due to its young years, compared to its much older legacy counterpart from the traditional financial world, combined with the more speculative nature of many crypto assets amplify this risk for every start-up and business participating in the ecosystem, no matter how big they are. In this realm, it's very unlikely that even the biggest of crypto companies will receive a government bailout if they collapse. The regulatory landscape here is more of a continuous patchwork of evolving policies and guidelines. Ever-changing regulatory guidelines and the lack of clear regulations pose even more challenges for crypto companies, particularly concerning compliance, legality of operations, and investor protection. Also, the rapid pace of technological change in blockchain and crypto technologies presents further opportunities and risks.

Stay Relevant

Projects must continually innovate to stay relevant, but this comes with the risk of untested technologies, scalability issues, and the constant threat of obsolescence. In such a world where assets are digital, security risks are Omnipresent. Not just hacks, frauds, or scams are significant risks as potential implications for asset security, investor confidence, and the project's credibility are too. Reason being "pumps and dumps," alongside the other factors, have made the retail community very weary about investing at first glance. Pumps and dumps are when a cryptocurrency is set up to have a large portion deliberately sold all at once, ensuring the seller a relatively large profit while drastically driving the price per token down, ruining the portfolios of all other owners. Human negligence and fraud have also proven themselves to be an existential threat to investors and the crypto industry's general reputation. 2023 alone showcased the downfall of the second largest exchange in the world "FTX" because of pure fraud, one of the most popular stablecoins in the industry "Terra Luna" due to miscalculations, the revolutionary yield generator destined to replace banks "Celcius" as it was a Ponzi scheme, and finally the stepping down of the father and CEO of Binance "CZ (Changpeng Zhao) as the exchange facilitated money laundering. It goes without saying that in the traditional financial world, such negative occurrences happen too, but the major difference in crypto is that due to the initial lack of taking this industry seriously on a whole, many start-ups experienced hyper-growth in very short periods of time without having the slightest idea how to structure themselves accordingly. As many companies weren't initially designed for this, once they scaled, cracks in the initial poor business model or simple neglect began to show, hence shining a spotlight on critical errors. Many founders tried to take advantage of this lack of accountability and confusion for some time, and some even still try today. Often, smaller companies in this industry that raise funds from retail investors simply disappear overnight with no refund nor accountability, resulting in the direct theft of users' funds. This direct lack of accountability coupled with a highly volatile and global playground has led to the abuse of the retail community. Because these negative events take place rather often, the retail community is far more exposed to financial loss on a regular basis than in the more classical option of stocks and bonds. Being such a novel sector of work, blockchain security firms, among others, present a great deal of risk too. As an example, some companies in the crypto security business that are very well known and audit literally every project and crypto company that has ended up either crashing, scamming, or being hacked. A lot of the companies claiming to be at the very peak of security, actually never had anything to do with real cyber security before Web3 to begin with! A well-hidden fact is that many of them inject millions of dollars into marketing and bluff their way to the top. As the majority of crypto CEOs and founders don't see through this velvety curtain of deception, they go with such security firms and end up being hacked for hundreds of millions of dollars, then pay the same security firms even more money to try and solve the problem they caused! This is another predominant yet unspoken form of risk in the crypto space. It's wise to do your own research on what the company did before Web3 plus the satisfaction rate of clients so you may find yourself a position in a great and ethical Web3 firm.

Custody of Funds

Another highly neglected risk segment in Web3 is the custody of the funds. Often delegated to other crypto companies throughout the industry, this possesses inherent risk exposure, unknown to the corporate brother. The Achilles heel of the entire crypto sector in my view are custodian companies. In essence, they are the crypto industry's version of banks but without the same level of security, compliance, insurance, and government backing. This itself is quite counterproductive as it just adds more layers of risk. Bitcoin was originally designed to be transferred and stored without any third parties. For every party you add, an extra layer of risk is added. Plus, people have already lost millions of dollars using such platforms, and even if they claim to have insurance, it could take forever to be refunded if worse goes to worst. Regardless of the faulty party, this small example goes to show just how risky the custodian companies are. Even with insurance, seldom will you recover the full amount after wasting months in a legal battle. The majority of even large crypto firms do use such platforms for custody of funds too, as they also provide somewhat of a digital interface for "managing" your digital assets. In essence, they're a custodian bank, which brings to the table custodian risk and bank risk, among more. One has to pose the question, "At its core, crypto is about owning and controlling your own digital assets and getting rid of the middleman, the bank. So why are we now using these new forms of banks in disguise?"

Assess the Risks

As you can see, while both the corporate and crypto worlds deal with risks and have some overlapping, the nature, magnitude, and management of these risks differ significantly. The corporate world, with its established practices and structures, offers a more predictable risk landscape and government and insurance backing if something goes wrong. In contrast, the crypto world, with its rapid innovation, evolving nature, and deceiving marketing facades, presents a more volatile and subtle risk environment. Understanding these differences is crucial for anyone navigating such sectors. It's about recognizing that risk, in all its forms, is a relative concept, shaped by the environment in which it exists. After careful analysis, it's evident that the crypto industry doesn't have the same business strategy and backing of its corporate twin. A wise man once said, "knowledge is knowing a tomato is a fruit, wisdom is knowing not to put it in a fruit salad." Here, it's paramount to not just know but to understand the nuances of working in crypto rather than a corporate job. Nobody wants to end up with a sour taste in their mouth because of a bad fruit salad.

This is something that can happen, as often you're directly accountable for everything for which you have been made responsible. The crypto realm, a mosaic of innovation and uncharted potential, happens to present a distinct skysill for employee accountability. This space, characterized by its pioneering spirit, demands a new kind of responsibility from its workforce, a responsibility that goes beyond conventional roles and embraces a broader, more impactful scope.

Reporting Lines and Corporate Structures

In the vast expanse of the corporate world, the concept of accountability for employees is a narrative interwoven with structure, predictability, and a guided sense of responsibility. This environment, unlike the free-roaming fields of crypto, is more akin to a well-charted map, where every path and boundary is defined and every role is marked with clear signposts of responsibility. In corporate settings, while employees are afforded a degree of autonomy, it is carefully balanced within the confines of established procedures and policies. Here, a lot like the regulations guiding the corporate world, freedom comes with a clear set of guidelines. Employees must navigate their roles, not as lone explorers but as members of a coordinated expedition, where every step aligns with the company's broader objectives. Unlike the decentralized decision-making often seen in crypto, corporate employees typically operate within a well-defined hierarchical structure. This structure, while potentially limiting in terms of independent decision-making, provides a safety net, ensuring that critical decisions are made with oversight and that the responsibility is shared rather than resting on a single individual's shoulders. This is why so many big companies are slow to implement new strategies but have been around for generations. This environment cultivates a culture where empowerment is managed. Employees are encouraged to take initiatives to some extent, but within the scope of their defined roles and responsibilities. This approach ensures that while innovation is fostered, it remains aligned with the company's strategic vision, thereby maintaining a balance between empowerment and accountability. Also, the ethical conduct of each individual employee forms the cornerstone of the legacy company's reputation. As we've seen a boom in cancel culture over recent times, this is something that's much more predominant in the corporate sector too. You don't want to push too much against the tide and are usually better off not to share any out of the box ideas, even when employees lend a hand and sometimes help out with other employees from completely different roles and responsibilities. However, unlike in the crypto space, these responsibilities are typically well-defined and come with a clear set of expectations. Moreover, if you don't execute well in these extra tasks, seldom will you be penalized. In the corporate world, accountability isn't closely tied to performance, apart from the more senior-level job positions, as that sector has more bandwidth for minor errors. Occasional failures or lapses in execution can sometimes lead to small consequences, usually concerning the loss of bonuses. This system, rather tolerant, ensures a low-to-medium level of accountability and a medium standard of performance all year round.

On the other side of the spectrum lies our digital twin, bouncing off a famous quote from Spider-Mman: "With great power comes great responsibility," well here "With great freedom comes great accountability." In the world of crypto, the freedom and autonomy afforded to employees come with an increased price of accountability. Each team member, often working remotely or in decentralized teams, must not only manage their workload but also ensure that their contributions align seamlessly with the project's overall objectives. Unlike its corporate twin, this level of autonomy bestowed upon employees in the crypto world requires a disciplined, entrepreneurial attitude, where one is constantly self-evaluating and adjusting to meet the ever-evolving needs of the company and market. The fluidity of roles in crypto projects will often place you in situations where you must make critical decisions independently.

Without the traditional hierarchies guiding each step, in the crypto space frequently you'll find yourself at the crossroads of significant project decisions. This environment cultivates a culture of empowerment but also demands a mature understanding of the company's vision and a deep sense of accountability for each decision made. This level of accountability and responsibility is usually the by-product of the company's general culture and management style. In a sector that is still striving to build trust and legitimacy, the ethical conduct of each employee becomes capital to the company's success. Each team member must not only adhere to the highest standards of honesty and transparency but also actively contribute to fostering a culture of integrity within the project and team. This commitment to ethical behavior extends beyond mere compliance; it's about being a steward of trust in a space where reputation is invaluable. Given the significant role of community and investor relations in the crypto space, trust is an invaluable asset to have in one's arsenal of tools. Moreover, the ability to communicate openly, accurately, and transparently is crucial for every employee. This responsibility involves more than just sharing progress or some updates; it's about pure transparency and commitment, addressing concerns, and building a relationship of trust with the wider community. No matter what crypto company you work for, they will likely have investors to whom they owe results. Within your company and respective role, you will have priorities and tasks, which will keep on accumulating if you're performing reasonably well. This is a sign of trust that will keep on growing as you keep performing well. Now, even if this is a good thing, you need to keep an eye on your role's main tasks. You can get overwhelmed rather quickly if you keep saying yes to new tasks, this is a blessing and a curse. If for some reason you perform poorly on one of the accepted tasks, you're 100% accountable, even if you have 20 other tasks on your plate and you accepted this one simply to try and help. Such failures can result in losing bonuses, stock options, or even getting fired on the spot, depending on the gravity of the situation. Individual employee accountability in the crypto industry is a dynamic and multi-faceted concept. It encompasses a blend of autonomy, ethical responsibility, adaptability, and community engagement. Every single one of your actions and decisions not only impacts the immediate project but also contributes to the broader narrative of the crypto industry. In this emergent and exciting sector, you're not just part of a crypto company; you're part of a high-level sports team, with everybody counting on each other. Always remember, if a player isn't performing terribly well or keeps on making mistakes, then they can be put on the bench, or simply kicked from the team and replaced; in short, it's up or out! To avoid this, make sure every task you need to complete, no matter how small or insignificant it may seem, is completed with the utmost transparency and efficiency possible. Be that star team player that everyone admires!

Risk and accountability aren't the only diverging points of the employment landscapes between the corporate and cryptocurrency sectors. The structure of rewards and incentives in the corporate and cryptocurrency sectors differs significantly, painting a vivid picture of stability vs. dynamism. Together, we'll now explore the contrasting reward systems inherent in these two distinct worlds, unravelling the nuances that define and differentiate them.

In the corporate sphere, the reward system is akin to a well-established road, marked with clear signposts and milestones. This environment offers predictability and a sense of long-term security in terms of compensation and benefits. Corporate employees typically enjoy structured salary packages, often accompanied by traditional benefits such as health insurance, retirement plans, and paid vacation. These perks are very often taken for granted and are usually a big part of the employee package. This structured approach provides a steady yet predictable income and career, offering financial stability and long-term security hence making the corporate world a very pragmatic choice for the majority of job hunters. Of course, in addition to base salaries, corporate reward systems often include performance-based bonuses. These bonuses, while contingent on meeting specific targets, are usually defined within a clear framework agreed upon beforehand or negotiated through the syndicate, providing a tangible incentive for achieving corporate goals. Often, the base salary and security of the corporate position supersede the potential of earning tremendous bonuses. Seldom do you earn three times your base salary if you hit or even surpass your targets. This said, the corporate world offers a ladder of progression, with promotions and career advancement tied to tenure, experience, and company commitment. Big promotions can, however, take many years, often requiring a lot of sacrifices from your personal and family life. This means putting to one side the holiday time and constantly being in the office making yourself noticeable by management over the years. Such a structured path of advancement provides you with clear goals, a pristine roadmap for stable professional growth, and a guaranteed mortgage from your banker!

By contrast, a job in the crypto realm presents reward systems that are as dynamic and fluid as the industry itself, thus making the rewards far greater than in the corporate world. This environment is characterized by flexibility, potential for high returns, and an element of risk. In the crypto world, compensation often includes a base salary, complemented by more variable components like performance-based commissions, tokens, stock options or even equity. These models offer the potential for significant returns, especially if the project/crypto company succeeds, but also come with a higher risk compared to the more predictable corporate salary structures. The reward system in crypto is closely tied to project performance and market dynamics. You may receive bonuses or token allocations based on the success of the project or the appreciation of the token value, providing an incentive structure that is directly linked to the success of the project/company. These perks, among many, need to be carefully evaluated as their value may increase or decrease drastically in a heartbeat, heavily affecting your income. Many people have, however, made over ten times their base salary in one month, and it's really not rare to obtain double figures for your monthly salary if you hit all of your targets. The fast-paced nature of the crypto industry can also lead to rapid role evolution and quick progression, furthermore positively impacting your salary. For those who thrive in such dynamic environments, the potential for rapid professional growth and significant financial rewards can be much higher compared to the more gradual progression typical in the corporate world. Again, it's not uncommon to be promoted after a few months within a crypto company structure if you fulfil your duties accordingly. You can even take on a C-level position if you play your cards right!

In comparison, the corporate world offers stability and predictability, while the crypto sector provides dynamism and the potential for significant gains. However, this dynamism comes with a higher degree of uncertainty and risk. These components are intricate to the crypto sector and are what really separates them from the corporate world. This dynamic and high-risk-reward environment is what drives the entire sector and makes it attractive to so many people all over the world. This space invites those willing to embrace risk with the allure of potentially far higher returns and rapid career advancement. This dichotomy presents a choice: the security of the known vs. the excitement and potential of the new frontier. For many, the ideal path may lie in finding a balance that aligns with their personal risk tolerance, career goals, and financial aspirations. For those with an urge to push the boundaries of the known and explore new heights, a crypto career is for you!

CHAPTER 3

Types of Jobs in Web3

One of the most important parts of your journey in working within the crypto field is understanding the types of jobs that are available and which jobs you'll be most successful at. This involves not just understanding the diversity of the Web3 job market and roles involved but, also equally importantly, the ones that are best suited for you. Often, I've spoken with recruitment agencies through my line of work, and they all say that so many individuals from the traditional job market are contacting them to find them a job position in Web3, and as this industry grows, so will the positions and candidates.

There are youngsters freshly out of university, college dropouts with a sweet tooth for crypto, all the way up to seasoned C-levels looking to quit their well-paid corporate jobs and settle for far smaller paychecks, just to get their feet through the door! Due to such a high demand of individuals wanting to work in this industry, the competition can be hard! Recruitment agencies are also tasked by crypto companies with searching for specific characteristics in future employees prior to signing any contracts. Naturally, the Web3 industry is heavily dominated by start-ups, and to work in such an environment requires a very special mindset in comparison with the traditional corporate world.

This chapter will showcase the types of crypto jobs people don't know about, but may be eligible to work in.

A. Rees-Evans, *So You Want to Work in Crypto*, https://doi.org/10.1007/979-8-8688-0503-5_3

A Look Back at History

Inaugurating this chapter is a brief segment on the history of start-ups to provide you further insight on what type of remote jobs await you on the other side. Throughout the entire twentieth century, the corporate world was hegemonized by the classical business model, hence characterized by stability and predictability. The start-up culture made its first appearance in the late 1970s as a new generation of entrepreneurs began to emerge, driven by a new ideology filled with revolutionary aspirations. The release of the Internet in 1969 was a salient driving factor of this new mindset, creating a fast-moving, dynamic environment and enabling the new generation of entrepreneurs to challenge traditional business models. Thanks to this new cross-border tool, creating and developing businesses became cheaper, faster, and more efficient. All of a sudden, instead of paying for expensive plane tickets and spending days, if not weeks, to discuss an idea with a foreign investor or clients, such opportunities became tangible from the comfort of their own homes (The history of startups From early days to today - FasterCapital).

Furthermore, access to large corporations was made possible to those of whom were simply not capable of financing such endeavors. The tables were levelled. As the Internet became more and more sophisticated, individuals were capable of communicating with almost anyone at any time. Scalability of companies relished many benefits of this tool also, capacitating international success while decreasing the time required to do so. As the late Charlie Chaplin emphasized in his speech in The Great Dictator, technology has indeed brought us closer together, while he also argues that it has driven our souls further away. Without a doubt, the Internet boom brought possibility and opportunity to those who sought it most, creating a new business era open to anyone, anywhere, to explore.

Due to the decentralized nature of the Internet, it shaped the landscape of traditional employee jobs. In 1979, IBM experimented with this very concept by allowing five of their employees needing a phone to complete their work tasks and to work remotely from home using the telephone. This became known as "Telecommuting." This method proved to be of great efficiency, so much so that by the year 1983, the initial team of five remote workers grew to a team of over two thousand! Since the last decade alone, there has been a rise of 115% in remote telecommuting. According to a Gartner survey, over 70% of all businesses are considering remote work for their employees since the Covid lockdowns.

On August 6, 1991, the first website ever going by the name of the "World Wide Web Project" went live (A Look Back At The Very First Website Ever Launched, 30 Years Later | WUNC), providing a whole new scope of possibilities for the Internet. Websites quickly became the new storefronts of start-ups building from their basements. With this futuristic tool, anyone could promote their business and content across all borders without renting a single store.

Since then, Wi-Fi and more sophisticated communication tools such as Zoom, Google Meets, and Microsoft Teams, among others, have further enhanced cross-border communications. Today, it's possible to have a live video call with someone on the other side of the world with no delays! These tools have taken remote work to the next level and enabled start-ups to hire and operate across the globe, 100% remotely. Many Web3 companies leverage these tools to create a very diverse team with special skill sets, providing them the luxury of working with exceptionally talented people.

As we now know, the Internet accelerated everything, from creating a business to client outreach all the way up to the direct scalability of companies. Start-ups are characterized by these unique traits. Blockchain technology is a next-level accelerator. You may make a cross-border payment using cryptocurrency in a few seconds, shaving days if not weeks off the normal banking fulfilment time. As both of these high-paced sectors meld together, the speed and reactiveness of the working environment increase in tandem.

Working in Web3 is a very, very unique job environment. The start-ups composing the majority of the companies in this industry are constantly adapting, pivoting to stay ahead of trends and regulations. You may experience waking up in the morning and the entire agenda of the company has been flipped on its head! You may be asked to complete a specific task and, during the execution of it, asked to stop and do something completely irrelevant and different. This is a start-up environment on steroids. If you like fast-paced, ever-changing environments, you will probably experience some of the best days of your entire working career. If you strive to push your limits day in and day out and find hypergrowth exciting, this industry is for you. For those who aren't particularly comfortable with constant change and prefer a more stable environment, you must prepare yourselves mentally for this working environment. Regardless of the job, role, or title you'll have, change will become a normal part of a day's work. As you embrace these tides of constant change, you'll grow into a stronger, more satisfied version of yourself, taking your professional career to the next level.

There are a very diverse and exciting range of roles in the Web3 ecosystem. You don't have to be a blockchain engineer or a trader to work in this industry. This is why almost anybody today can get a job in crypto! Many Web3 companies are keen to give new entrants a shot. Think of it as a new country being built. They're constantly growing, and because it's an extremely diverse ecosystem, it's an extremely diverse job market.

For example, if you've been an investment banker, you're probably going to be a great fit on the OTC (Over the Counter) desks in some private structures out of Dubai or Switzerland. On the other hand, if you've been a high school math teacher, it's probably best to target a trading platform in a start-up and work on developing some new algorithms once you've digested a few books on the matter. Your enjoyment of your new Web3 career will be determined by how well your skills, experience, and personality fit with the specific role that you've chosen to do.

To provide a spectrum of thought on what jobs typically have openings to newcomers, let's now explore some detailed examples in the following sections.

CEXs (Centralized Exchanges)

CEXs (Glossary 8) are the Web3 version of the Wall Street stock exchanges in New York. These are the main gateways in between Web2 and Web3. They're the On-Off ramps where multiple cryptos are also exchanged. The majority of them have hundreds of millions, if not billions, of dollars worth of assets under management (AUM) and in daily trading volume. As crypto has greatly evolved over the years, there's not just Bitcoin or Ethereum out there anymore. There are thousands and thousands of different tokens called Altcoins, all looking for an exchange to be traded publicly. In CEXs they have lawyers, operation specialists, traders, financial experts, HR teams, sales teams, account managers, partnership managers, developers, marketing experts, graphic designers, copywriters, and accountants. There are a few more that can be added, but that's the bulk of which a CEX needs to function.

They're a great place to target for your first job as they fire and hire often, so they're always on the lookout for new talent!

Web3 Marketing Companies

Regardless of the industry, you always need marketing. There are some very large Web3 marketing companies out there, and they specialize in brand awareness, token launch marketing, NFT marketing campaigns, and global "go to market" strategies. These guys also partner up with really big Web2 brands like L'Oréal, Ubisoft, football clubs, and big artists looking to roll out their new set of NFTs. Every single company in Web3 and Web2 needs marketing. Big Web3 marketing firms are often very busy due to this high demand for their services, yet there are a lot of them out there, so the competition between them is fierce. Usually, Web3 companies are composed of experienced PR and marketing experts, lawyers, HR teams, account managers, graphic designers, copywriters, operation specialists, partnership developers, business developers, and sales managers.

Depending on your original background, Web3 marketing companies can be an excellent way to onboard in the industry.

31

Market Makers

Intrinsically connected to CEXs, DEXs liquidity providers, and projects, they're an essential part of the ecosystem. To simplify, they're in the middle of every transaction and fulfilling the orders of traders wishing to buy or sell tokens. Without a market maker helping a project's live and tradable tokens, it can make life really tough to actually buy or sell the tokens with a trading strategy as the spreads will be large and pricing quite volatile. They help keep the spreads tight and the trading charts smooth. Market makers have big teams of traders, lawyers, PR teams, developers, algorithm specialists, HR teams (depending on the size), sales teams, account managers, business developers, and partnership developers.

If you have a strong mathematical background and have a decent understanding of trading, this may be a great choice to start your journey in Web3.

Web3 Recruitment Agencies

Web3 recruitment agencies play an essential part in supporting the scalability of this industry. They help spot talent and match them with the big crypto companies that are constantly growing. On top of this, because they're connected to so many entities, the majority actually even help raise funds, create partnerships, and much more! Due to the growth of this industry, the Web3 recruitment agencies are flooded with demand and often hire new employees themselves as they need big teams on the backend to meet the demand. Commonly, you'll find big HR teams, talent acquisition specialists, business developers, accountants, and assistants.

This is a great option for those of you from the traditional job sectors, such as secretaries, talent agents, etc., enabling you to get involved in Web3 without going full on Degen.

Crypto Event Organizations

A classic example of how the normal world and Web3 can blend together. Crypto events are huge in this industry, and they're all over the world, all the time. They bring huge Key Opinion Leaders (KOLs - Glossary 8), celebrities, politicians, whales, start-ups, service providers, and investors all together in the same place at the same time. They organize great segments such as pitch competitions, influential debates, networking rooms, and crazy side events with the wildest parties out there! They have huge partnerships with a lot of the titans in Web3, enabling them to be very well respected by all in the industry. These organizations need lawyers, accountants, big teams of business developers, partnership contractors, operational teams, HR teams, marketing teams, PR teams, copywriters, graphic designers, and sales teams.

For any person with some festival and/or event background, this is definitely the type of company you should reach out to, as they look to hire experienced people to help further develop their growth in Web3.

Web3 Media Outlets

Unlike Peter Parker, you won't get paid for a pretty picture of Spider-Man; however, Web3 newspapers provide all of the info on what's hot and what's not. The new trends, new best tech, projects, and even all of the regulatory news concerning the SEC, data protection with the GDPR, politics, therefore influencing the industry and covering big events too! The largest Web3 newspapers even have accelerator programs, investment programs, and grants, of which they provide promising projects with great potential. As you've probably noticed by now, the majority of the "Traditional" style Web3 companies actually have a lot more going on in the background than what originally meets the eye. These companies need big teams of journalists with a passion for crypto, lawyers, business developers, editors, partnership experts, sales teams, account managers, and accountants.

It's a great place to get involved in crypto if you have a literary background, noting that sometimes you can even sign up with them as a freelancer to start!

Investment Funds

Investors, VCs, and angels are the oxygen of Web3; without them, projects don't get funding, innovation comes to a halt, and the whole ecosystem grinds to a slow stop. The majority of them did get wiped out during this bear market (2022–2023), and now there's only very serious players taking on this role. They're extremely cautious and careful prior to placing any funding; they verify the market caps, tokenomics, partnerships, teams, token/equity price, scalability, and moreover, how they'll get their ROI back. It's a really exciting place to be in the crypto world as you're at the very forefront of innovation. You're deciding which projects will be the next unicorns and hearing pitches from people all over the world trying to build the next big thing. You have the power to actually shape the future of the entire sector; it's an extremely powerful position to be in. In investment funds, usually you have analytics specialists, lawyers, investor relation managers, accountants, business developers, and operational C-levels.

This is a really good choice for those of you with a strong mathematical or economic background with a reasonable understanding of blockchain and how the industry works.

Token Projects

The beating hearts of the industry are the projects trying to build the future with crazy clever ideas. These are often bootstrapped to start with and propose, at the early stages, big shares of equity and/or tokens. At the start, they're always looking for funds, negotiating with VCs and investors, trying to raise a few million dollars. Projects promise decent salaries too, but only once they're funded. The risk factor with this company choice is rather high; however, so are the rewards if everything goes according to plan. You can literally be a majority holder of the next Dogecoin and get a C-level position! However, I do insist on doing your research in depth prior to onboarding with them because they ask a lot of work from you with very little pay at the beginning, and the chances of real success are quite low. Projects need advisors, crypto enthusiasts willing to work big hours, a CMO, CEO, COO, or CTO to start, and then once funded, the sky's the limit. Soon after the fundraise, they also hire sales teams, account managers, lawyers, business developers, partnership managers, and development teams. Projects are a great place to start just to get some experience, and if everything goes well, retire a couple of years later.

Ambassadors

All types of Web3 companies have teams of them promising commissions for every deal they bring to the table, of which they're able to close. Commission percentages range on the type of company you're an ambassador for but also on how many deals you've brought to them they've been able to close. Many times, ambassadors are in the Telegram groups hunting for new potential clients to send to the companies they've contracted with. It's quite frequent that ambassadors have these types of free-lance contracts with a variety of different companies from different sectors simultaneously. This way, they can always find a match in their portfolio and cross-reference. Ambassadors operate individually and work remotely. You're completely free of any employee/employer obligations, so it's quite an attractive job for a lot of side hustlers, even if people do this full-time too. If you do want to do this to make a living, it does help to have a big crypto network; if not, it's still possible, but just a lot of work diving through telegram groups all day looking for the right match. If you're looking for an easy way to test the waters in Web3, this is a guaranteed option. You can contact any crypto company and ask for the ambassador referral contract directly via LinkedIn, their email, or other relative employees contact details, including the Telegram groups directly.

35

Community Managers

Even if AI is making life tough for moderators at this moment, it can never replace them fully as they can, if required, hop on calls with clients to help resolve issues. In short, community managers and moderators are in the Telegram groups for the most of their time explaining, helping, and resolving project/client-related issues. They're in essence the live service line you contact when you have a question or problem about that particular company or product. Very often, they're extremely important in the early days of projects prior to their token launch, reassuring community members and answering some launch-related questions like when's the Initial Dex Offering (IDO - Glossary 10), where can they buy the simple agreement for future tokens (SAFT - Glossary 11), etc.... It's always useful to speak at least two or three languages and have a little knowledge of crypto terms and acronyms. The community asking you questions is from all over the globe, speaking a lot of different languages, and enquiring about some precise information concerning the product/service of the company you're working for.

If you don't have any big fancy diplomas and love helping people, this is a great place to kick off your career in Web3, noting that literally all companies in Web3 hire community managers.

Blockchain Developers

This one may seem quite obvious; however, new blockchains and codes are emerging constantly, making it extremely hard for even the most experienced of developers to keep up. These extremely gifted individuals are the architects of this ever-expanding industry. Every time a new blockchain is released, it requires talented individuals to master the undermining code to such a level that they can build applications on top of it without any interoperability problems. Because there's an ongoing flow of new blockchains, each possessing unique styles and features of code, developers don't necessarily have the bandwidth to learn the intricacies of every new one that appears. This leaves open doors to any developers willing to spend the time to master the code. There's always a shortage of talented developers in the industry, and there can never be enough.

If you have IT experience and some extensive coding knowledge, you may be able to master a newly released blockchain and charge a pretty penny for your development services!

Lawyers

Forever surrounded by regulatory uncertainty, the entire industry is in dire need of lawyers who can help navigate these hindrances. It's important to note that legal opinions are needed in almost every single company in Web3, be it for compliance reasons, contract amendments, fiscal structures, or client advisory. Not only do lawyers have the option to work in almost any company in this industry, they can also be the necessary bridge from the corporate world to Web3. As of 2023, tokenization of Real World Assets (RWA) has become a hot topic. Of course, we're talking about assets from the real world, such as hotels, apartments, gold, oil, bonds, etc. Any asset you can think of is subject to becoming tokenized on the blockchain. The owners and managers of such assets rarely know where to turn to for such a transformation and often seek legal opinion from lawyers in this space to help them overcome these uncertainties. It's not uncommon for the lawyer to introduce them to well-established third parties to help them handle the technology side of the transformation as well.

Any regulated lawyer may strive to enter this space after bringing themselves up to speed with the most relevant topics and regulatory framework.

Now, of course, there are far more jobs and sectors in Web3 than the twelve cited above, such as social media managers, presenters, or even motion graphic designers, among many more; however these are very often the starting places, allowing people from traditional jobs to seamlessly enter the Web3 working space. These job types usually lead to great growth and, more importantly, build up that dense crypto knowledge you need to fully understand and operate within the industry. They even help you develop a very deep network of important and influential people in the space in order to become a very valuable asset to any major crypto firm and obtain a C-level position.

Determining Your Profile

As you're deciding which job type would fit you most, it's key to determine what your profile is. For starters, we know the Web3 industry can be very demanding and intense; you need to make sure that you will have a deep, passionate drive for your future role and company. It's capital that you're genuinely excited about your job when you wake up every morning, as your passion and drive for your role will be necessary to get you through the long hours, complexities, and challenges this industry can have. It is necessary to receive a sense of fulfilment thanks to the value you will provide from your position. A perfect job fit will help reduce stress and depression, enable you to express your inner passions, provide a deep sense of meaning, and reinforce your personal values, all of which will bring joy and fulfilment not just to your professional life but your personal life too.

Personality plays a major part in determining what job you will be good at and which ones just simply aren't a match. The immutable characteristics making you, you, are to be highly considered as you search for their dream job in Web3. If overlooked, this may result in finding a job, but promoting an overall bad experience in Web3 as your job simply didn't match your own unique traits. Henceforth, prior to actively searching for any old job in Web3 you think may tick all of the above, there are a few things you may do to discover what type of jobs your personality and traits may fit. The following sections provide some highly recommended guidelines to follow to enhance your chances of finding a perfect job match (How To Find the Perfect Job For You (With Tips and Tricks) | Indeed.com).

The Good

Create a list of your interests, personality type (extrovert/introvert), qualifications, and what you're naturally good at; this is the perfect place to start. Painting the tapestry of your natural gifts will help keep you on the right track as you job hunt. Once you have a helicopter view of these, a common sense of direction should be revealed. As an example, if you graduated in economics, are interested in American politics, are naturally good with people, and are an extrovert, you may want to seek a position in public relations of a large CEX in the United States.

The Bad

Write down the negative points about your current job. As you delve deep into the intricacies of the down sides of your current position and company, you will be laying down key metrics on which must be avoided in your future endeavors. The goal of changing jobs, never mind the industry, is to improve on what you currently have. Often, as you freely write down the negatives of your ongoing position, a few unexpected downsides you didn't necessarily think of will pop out all of a sudden. It's capital to capture them in written form so not to lose or forget, then to find them in your new position in Web3.

Pick a Winner

Find out what companies you'd like to work for. Thousands of companies exist in Web3, ranging from early ventures to more established start-ups pioneering the industry. If you desire to work in Web3 solely to work for one particular company, that's perfectly fine, and you must arm yourself with the skill set necessary to obtain your goal. If you don't have any specific company in mind, do some market research and see which companies spark your interest. In both cases, check for employee reviews on recruitment sites as they provide valuable insights as to what their experience was like, which may help you confirm your choice, or in some rare cases, dodge a bullet. Either way, be sure to keep an open mind, as often when you start in Web3, you may have to take a temporary position in a different company and position just to get your foot through the door. If this is the case, leverage such an opportunity as a trampoline to take you to the next level whilst gaining valuable industry knowledge, further increasing your value to employers.

Make Connections

Connect with individuals working in the position you want. Don't be afraid to reach out to those in positions similar to the ones you wish to occupy. Social media channels may be an easy way to connect with them, especially LinkedIn, as you may curate your search through the filters, enabling you to connect with many individuals in that exact position you're thinking of. For example, if you want to be a business developer in a Web3 marketing agency, try searching for Web3 marketing agencies, then scanning their employees until you reach the relevant ones to add as friends. Speaking with people in your dream position will not only provide valuable feedback as to what it's like but also give you insight into how they made it there, which may be a significant addition to your strategic arsenal.

Personality Test

Something as important as choosing a new job merits a few minutes of fine-tuning your own self-awareness. Although you may already feel confident in knowing who you are, taking a personality test can prove to not just confirm but also reveal some interesting aspects you may not have given much thought to! Personality tests such as the Myers-Briggs test can help give you that extra slice of information, further curating the best possible job and career path.

Never Give Up

Year on year there's an increase of approximately 80% of individuals working in Web3 (Number of people working in blockchain space climbs almost 80% year-on-year (finbold.com)), noting the industry is still rather new and underdeveloped, the demand to work in this space will only increase as time goes on. Of course, this means that competition for job positions is highly competitive, and finding a job can require some time. If you truly are passionate about working in Web3, never stop applying for jobs. After each rejection, ask for candid feedback, which will allow you to self-correct and increase the chances of your next interview. Also, don't be afraid to apply to as many relevant open positions as possible, even if that means sending hundreds of CVs. If getting your foot through the door turns out harder than expected, you can always start at a lower level then work your way up. Finally, do apply for the same job again and again, even if you've been rejected multiple times before. I've seen people in that exact situation be hired after multiple rejections, just because they demonstrated extreme determination.

Summary

Choosing the perfect job in Web3 can be challenging; another quick tip is to look for direct crossovers from your current position to the closest position available. For example, in the corporate world, we have project managers; in Web3, we have Scrum masters and product owners. Applying for a cross over job after having bulked up on your crypto knowledge should unveil a far easier transition into Web3. As long as your long-term goals may be achieved, feel free to start your journey in this industry with any welcoming job position welcoming you. However, if you're not 100% satisfied and are below your pay grade, do not dwindle in that position. Leverage the connections you'll make to take you to the next level. Once you're in the industry and have a relevant network, switching to your dream job becomes much easier with far less hassle. Even if it may take some time, once you're in the right job at the right company, you'll never look back.

Just remember that the struggles you may encounter finding your dream job will only be temporary; even if they persist for a week, a month, or even a year, you will end up where you want to be.

CHAPTER 4

Preparing for the Right Crypto Job

One of the most important days you will ever have in your Web3 career is the day of your job interview. It's a completely different ball game in comparison to a traditional job interview. Here, the interviewers can be professionals or just some experienced employees from the company with no formal recruitment training. Due to the naturally dynamic rhythm of the Web3 industry, often those facing you during your interview are very busy and don't have the luxury of time or patience.

Considering other factors such as bandwidth, specific criteria, and fatigue, seldom are your interviewers capable of spending hours on a call with you or explaining the same thing over and over again. In many large crypto firms, turnover is key, and the same goes for the hiring frequency. On top of the above unique traits of the Web3 hiring style, it's important to note that they do offer chances to those who seek and opportunities to those who aspire potential.

As this industry is young, yet growing greatly day after day, there's a dire need to hire more and more talented individuals. This is one of the most inordinate pain points of the entire industry hiring talented people with experience. Also, as the industry is young, finding talented individuals with experience can be quite a challenge! With this lack of adequate talent, a window of opportunity is omnipresent, enabling more or less anyone to have a chance at working in the industry.

© Alexander Rees-Evans 2024
A. Rees-Evans, *So You Want to Work in Crypto*,
https://doi.org/10.1007/979-8-8688-0503-5_4

In this chapter, we'll review three key factors to help you find the best crypto fit:

- Your crypto CV

- Selecting potential candidates

- Interviewing

Building a Crypto CV

To have an optimum chance of working in Web3, one of the most important elements you will need to rise to perfection is your CV Recruiters view hundreds of CVs every single week, so it's important to ensure that yours has the edge. As per the adage, "You only get one chance to make a first impression, and yours may be in the hands of the secretary." In our context, this means that prior to any interview, you need to impress the person judging your CV In Web3, the person receiving your CV is the gatekeeper to your interview. Even if that particular individual is indeed the secretary and is solely tasked with organizing the CVs before HR scrutinizes them, that secretary is the first person you need to impress. One may even classify this as "getting past the gatekeeper." Furthermore, not all recruiters are there to find you a job, but to fill a position, you need to impress. Regardless of the industry, you will always have what is known as a gatekeeper. A gatekeeper is an individual who stands between yourself and the main person you wish to speak with, the decision maker. In our case, the gatekeeper is the initial receiver of your CV, and the decision maker is the individual who decides whether or not to hire you. Even if the person receiving your CV isn't the decision maker, they have the power as the gatekeeper to say yes or no to allow you to communicate with the decision maker. You must treat gatekeepers with the utmost respect in order to get to the next stage of the interview process. Henceforth, a well-structured CV is capital to capture their attention, thus opening a line of communication. Bearing in mind that the gatekeepers and decision makers receive a staggering amount of them from individuals located all over the world. As one passes on their CV, it's capital to make it as clear, professional, grammatically correct, and stand out as much as possible. Your CV must reflect not only your qualifications, skill set, past jobs, or achievements, but also your work ethics.

Take this normal, basic CV with no colors nor passion involved (Figure 4-1); immediately, your impression is that the issuer isn't special.

James Smith

LinkedIn: www.linkedin.com/in/james smith | Email: Jamessmith@gmail.com | Telegram: @jamessmith

Work Experience

BD and Sales at Nike   May 2022 – Present

• Led the pivot from a product with no PMF to agency business model.
• Created a service offering and generated close to mid-six figures in revenue (started at $0).
• Launched projects other international brands and agencies.
• Created and optimized agency processes (discovery, development, delivery) and cross-functional communication.

Business Development at Samsung   Oct 2021 – May 2022

• Contributed to growth of sales in the USA (15 million per month to 400 million in 5 months).
• Onboarded 4 major KOLs and 10+ smaller partners in the CIS region.
• Planned and implemented user acquisition campaigns for partners on YouTube and Telegram.
• Helped launch retention and activation email marketing campaigns.

Startup Success Manager at Techstars   Nov 2020- Feb 2022

• Oversaw 4 investments: 1 frozen, 2 failures, 1 success (an innovative residential property management company that grew to over 1.5 million sq. meters under management in 2 years).
• Coordinated and contributed to budget, strategy, and team formation to ensure startups viability.
• Did legal work and contract negotiations.

Traditional finance, entrepreneurial endeavors, trading career   2017-2020

Started my career as an analyst at a hedge fund and grew to be a trader assistant. After leaving Then I left and tried launching business projects and creating YouTube content. Later I joined a car dealership selling emblematic Soviet 4x4 vehicles to wealthy individuals in Mexico and sourced and helped close the biggest B2B deal (sold 19 cars to a resort operator). I traded US stocks for 1.5 years with my own capital and learned a lot of lessons.

Education

European University   Oct 2014-Sept 2016

Bachelor of Science, Finance Geneva, Switzerland Graduated with Summa Cum Laude (GPA: 3.9/4.0).
President of the Student Board for 2015-2016 academic year.

Languages

English, Russian, Spanish, French

Figure 4-1. *Generic CV*

Here, we can see a very bland, boring document, not justifying just how qualified this individual may be. At first glance, it doesn't inspire much, nor does it create enthusiasm on behalf of the hiring team.

Now, if we take the same information from this CV and restructure the entire document in a much fresher approach (Figure 4-2), we immediately see a difference.

Figure 4-2. *CV with pizazz*

With strong, bold colors, a professional photo, and engaging graphics, make your CV pop! Also, it's best to send your CV in two formats if possible, one in Word format and the other in PDF. Reason being, some recruiters remove your information before sending it to their client, which is your future potential boss.

Adecco Retail did a poll with over 1000 recruiters and discovered that it takes an employer only 34 seconds to decide if a CV is worth considering! That's all; your career goals, aspirations, and dreams are predetermined in 34 seconds by someone you've never even met (Ten tips on how to write the perfect CV | Work & careers | The Guardian). Cliches, lies, and typos are all just some of the reasons why people aren't offered interviews, in Web3, it's especially true. As one tailors their CV to the specific job they're looking for, the following factors will help provide guidance and structure, making sure the 34 seconds of the recruiter will be maximized:

- Relevance: For sure, you need to stand out; however, you must make sure that all of the content is relevant to the position you're looking for. This means making multiple CVs, each tweaked to target a specific role and job position. To develop your CVs in such a way, be sure to read multiple job offers and descriptions, obtain the general consensus of what features and profiles are required, then craft your CV adopting such relevance. It's capital not to lie, but rather to emphasize and expand on the desired skills and experience. In the words of David D'Souza, the membership director of the Chartered Institute of Personnel and Development, the professional HR body. "Look at the job description, and make sure that it's clear why you'll be able to deliver in that role."

- Wording: Don't be cliché; avoid using the same old words that the other nine hundred and ninety-nine CVs behold, such as "passionate," "hardworking," or "team player." Be unique and show your capacity to think outside of the box. Combine industry relevance with wording from the job descriptions, really matching the wording used to describe those job positions you're looking to obtain. Integrating words like "accountable," "purpose," "high achiever," and "honest" can also make a difference.

- Details: By nature, we tend to hold back and promote modesty over flamboyance, especially when it comes to promoting ourselves in the workplace. As one crafts their CV, withholding certain achievements or information to remain humble is a double-edged sword. Modesty is good, but showing what you're really capable of is also important; remember, you have 34 seconds to impress. Prior to shipping out your CV to recruiters, send it to a work colleague you trust who will provide valuable feedback and gauge if you're coming off too humble or too flamboyant.

- Size matters: Just because you can fill five pages doesn't mean you should. Just because you've worked for ten different companies, it doesn't mean they're all relevant. Condense all of your past experiences if you have a lot of them and make it super easy to understand. The more you add, the longer will be your CV, and the more relative information will be diluted. Be sure to make every word useful and get straight to the point. You're not writing your autobiography; you're showing with military precision and scope why you're the best person for the job.

- Spelling: Regardless of your origins, if you're applying for an English-speaking job, your CV needs to show that you're capable of it. Even native English people happen to make a spelling mistake from time to time, but none may be found on your CV. The same goes for grammar. Even if you use auto-correct as you draft it, it's better to be safe than sorry. Once ready, send it to some friends, colleagues, and family members; more often than not, you'll find a couple of details you'll need to modify.

- Be yourself: As recruiters pick up your CV, they need to get a feel of the type of person you are. May that be through fonts, writing style, choice of words, structure, graphics, or even colors. Promote your person through all of the above tools in order to get across your personality. Research color codes and meaning; for example, power colors are generally rich tones of dark black, red, blue, green, and brown (Power Colors (casualpower.com)). Honesty promoting colors are dark blue, scarlet, peach, and purple (4 Colors That Symbolize Honesty - PolishingColors.com). Be sure to play around with all of them and find which ones are a best fit for you.

- Photo: Photos aren't necessary but if you do, be sure to have a professional photographer take a business style photo of you. On average, such snapshots can cost around $30 USD and can be very useful for your professional career. Having a professional headshot can instantly make you look like an executive, further enhancing the belief that you're a fit for the specific role.

- Hobbies: Recruiters don't want to know that you go out for a drink every weekend as there's zero-value added stating this. Instead of using your hobbies as a generic segment, leverage them to promote your self-discipline and dedication. Transform "Weekend drinks with friends" into "Social relations building," transform "Walks with my dog" into "Canine education and health." Find clever, high-level ways of expressing what you spend your extra time doing, creating a high-level overview of a well-structured personal life on top of your professional one.

In the Web3 industry, often employers give specific characteristics to recruiters as to what traits they're looking for in their new employees. These characteristics are designed to filter out any unwanted personality types. For example, the general traits recruiters look for when hiring in Web3 are the following:

- Honesty: In a world without police, justice, or any real repercussions, from time to time employees venture down a dark path. It is industry knowledge that as an employee fulfils their daily tasks and engages with clients, clients try to negotiate on different terms, promising to send direct funds to the employee in exchange for a larger discount. Whether you're in the legal department, sales, accounting, or more, you will come across moments where individuals will approach and tempt you into accepting funds, favors or services in exchange for giving them something from the company you work for in return. Unfortunately, some employees do accept such bribes, hence why honesty plays a very big part in the recruitment process in Web3.

- Start-up experience: As we will learn in Chapter 6 of this book, the Web3 industry is one relevant to start-ups. Working in such an environment comes with its own unique set of challenges and features. Demonstrating that you have experience or are ready to operate in such a unique field of work will give confidence to the recruiters that you will be able to handle the job position you're applying for and the challenges bestowed upon you.

- Champion mentality: The Web3 world is akin to some of the most powerful start-ups, constantly striving to keep ahead of the competition. Many founders operating in Web3 believe that the employees must foster a sense of hyper achievement. Hiring such individuals will provide the company with, in short, a high-level sports team composed only of A players. Each company wants to have the best possible team, just like every major sports team desires and keeps only the best performers of that specific discipline. By showing exceptional sports, academic, or professional achievements, your champion mentality will be evident. Be sure to show something of this regard, even if it dates back to your childhood, as many founders believe that a champion mentality is developed during that period.

- Tenacity: During your career in this industry, you will face many challenges related to your direct role and the company's situation itself. A certain form of tenacity is required on your behalf to perform during such times. Also, your job will require ongoing dedication day in and day out. Closing deals, maintaining client relations, drafting legal documents, whatever your line of work may be, you will need to have a solid mind set to keep pursuing and performing.

Where to Look for Crypto Jobs

Once your CV is fully prepared and ready to impress the recruiters, you must now determine where to find jobs in Web3 and how to target the right ones for you. As you embark on your crypto job hunt, finding job openings can turn out to be quite the challenge. Strategizing and knowing where to look can help save a lot of time and energy. Whether you're targeting recruitment agencies, the companies directly, or recruitment websites, opportunities abound if your search is on par. Optimizing your job hunt will help accelerate your entry into the Web3 workforce. In this section, we'll take a look at some of the many places you can find job openings in Web3 and how to target them efficiently.

Social Circle

Opening the dance, we have a heavily overlooked option, your social circle. Never underestimate the power of your network, as your network truly is your net worth. This doesn't mean that you have friends already working in the industry, capable of handing you a job. It simply means that you can fire up your social networks, such as LinkedIn, Facebook, Instagram, Reddit, Discord, Telegram, or even X, and simply ask around. From experience, a lot of job positions in Web3 are filled through the social circle. There's even dedicated crypto groups on Telegram, solely designed for Web3 networking; the great news is that they're completely free to use and, with some luck, can get you in the heat of the action straight away. To find such specific groups, it's great to ask around on the other social networks to people already working in the industry.

Blogs

Another overlooked channel for recruitment is a blog. The Web3 industry thrives on personal branding, entrepreneurship, and sharing of information. Very different from the pixelated, isolated blogs we saw when we were in school, today's blogs are dense, informative, and very much in the public eye. So much so that even the most established of Web3 companies have one and provide regular updates within. Medium is one of the largest, most used blogs by the Web3 community and is easily accessible. Much like the LinkedIn search bar, here, you can also curate your search by entering specific words, helping refine the results. If you really want to get your name out there, it's completely possible to create your own Medium space and present yourself publicly to the community. By creating a well-structured personal blog, you may receive a pleasant surprise plus yield some unexpected messages from recruiters!

Recruitment Websites

Traditional recruitment websites are stepping up their game too. As the demand for talent in this industry keeps on rising, the larger Web3 companies need to onboard new employees at a high frequency. Having understood this demand, sites like Indeed, Glassdoor and Monster are catching up. Nowadays, it's not uncommon to find a large selection of Web3 related jobs on them once you've curated your search. If you're going to use these recruitment websites, be sure to recreate your entire profile and in-site CV. This may take some time, but once it's done, it can save you a lot of time, enabling you to browse and apply to a job in just a few clicks.

Websites like Cryptocurrencyjobs.co, Crypto.jobs, Web3.career, Cryptoblist.co, and Cryptocareers.io are just some of the specialized Web3 recruitment websites, solely dedicated to job openings in this industry. Though they may not be as nice as their Web2 twins from a UI/UX perspective, they often propose jobs from many small- and medium-sized Web3 companies, thus providing opportunities directly from the core of the sector. Often, the jobs posted on these more dedicated websites aren't available on the more classical recruitment websites, as discussed in the paragraph above.

Conferences

Crypto conferences, side events, and even virtual meetups in metaverses are also prime locations to job hunt. If you're able to physically go to conferences or side events, you'll be in the buzzing epicenter of the entire sector, with the possibility to engage directly with Web3 firms. Depending on the size of the conference, there can easily be a few hundred different yet relevant companies attending. Many of them will be in their expansion stage, hence looking to hire immediately or sometime in the near future. An in-person meeting in a dynamic social environment can definitely give you the edge over other candidates too. If you don't have the possibility of a physical meeting, there's also the option of targeting online meetings, Ask Me Anything (AMAs) on X, or even meet-ups in a metaverse! You can find times, contexts, and dates for such digital interactions in Telegram announcement channels of projects, posts on X, and shared information on Reddit.

Recruitment Agencies

It goes without saying that there's also recruitment agencies in this space who are usually tasked with recruiting for industry leaders such as Binance. Even if the industry leaders have their own portals for job applications, they outsource some of the heavy lifting to professional agencies to increase their talent pool. Some of the best Web3 talent agencies you can contact and send your CV to directly are Plexusrs. com, Cryptorecruit.com, Thecryptorecruiters.io, Prioritycrypto.jobs, and Blockchainheadhunter.com. You may reach out to such entities freely, and if they feel they can help, they will do so without asking for a fee on your behalf. However, just because they will help find a match doesn't mean you should delegate your entire job search altogether. Be sure to keep searching on your side, as agencies can get overwhelmed or simply forget about you after a while if they haven't found a match.

Headhunters

Lastly, one of the best options is to find a Web3 headhunter directly! You wouldn't believe how many recruiters turn to this after a while. In short, a headhunter is a recruiter that specializes in hunting/stealing key individuals from one company to another. Furthermore, they're generally open to helping you as they're heavily incentivized by commission they receive from employers every time they find a match. This is a big driving factor for many of them as if they don't find a match, they don't get bonuses, it's that simple. This economic model based highly on merit, incentivizes them to work long hours. They're also quite easy to find and engage with. LinkedIn is a pretty much guaranteed way of finding a myriad of eager headhunters. By typing "Web3 recruiter," "Crypto headhunter," "Web3 headhunter," etc., in the search bar, plenty of relative results should appear, all waiting for you to engage with them.

Acing Your Crypto Interview

Once your CV has been crafted and polished, your line of communication with recruiters open and successful, your next stage will be the interview itself. Depending on the type of outreach you did, whether it be via Telegram or a headhunter, the channel and type of reply may differ heavily. For these reasons, you must keep a keen eye on all channels used for your outreach at all times. This is another big difference from job hunting in the more traditional corporate sector, as never in a million years would a traditional recruiter contact you on Telegram to organize a video conference interview. In this realm, it can definitely happen, even if usually they'll send you an email. Keep a watch out though, as they can also call you on your mobile phone out of the blue. If you've been applying to job positions and have been hoping to receive a reply, make sure you check your mobile phone and voicemail too. A recruiter can call you from an unknown phone number at any given time of the day, and replying without thinking could cost you the job. For example, if you're in a very noisy place, having a bad day, or just completely focused on something, don't even reply. You must remember that if you choose to answer such a call, the very moment you answer, you will give your first impression. There are no second chances on making a first impression, and if you can't create a stellar impression at the moment they call you, it's preferable to not answer and call back at a more suitable time. First impressions count. If you do receive such a call, generally speaking, it will just be an introduction call, asking if you'd be available for a more formal interview. As you validate the time and date of your interview, be sure to ask what time zone and video conference tool (Zoom, etc.) you'll be using. Depending on the size of the company, fixed dates and times may be pre-established for the interview, meaning that you have to move your schedule to fit them, not the other way around. There's even the possibility of having a group interview with other individuals at the same time!

Web3 interviews are primarily stages composed of three steps: The preliminary interview, final interview, tests. These three steps aren't necessarily mandatory but just the norm. If you're applying for a position in a small to medium sized start-up (10–60 employees), you probably won't have the test stage. Regardless of which stage of the interview you're at, the following 18 steps will help you prepare for every single one of them starting with your preparation before the interview:

1) Know the company. There's nothing more discouraging for an interviewer than obtaining a void of silence when the applicant can't develop on the company or its history. Don't be that person; take a couple of minutes reviewing the company, their main products, services, competitors, and Unique Selling Propositions (USPs Glossary 12). Show the interviewer/s that you've done your

homework and are up to speed with the company's latest trends. Be sure to know enough about the company to be able to have a conversation about why you would fit in and what extra value you bring to the table. It's also great if you can ask some questions about what you've researched, as this demonstrates without a doubt that you have indeed put in the effort to prepare for the interview.

2) Revise the job description. Reading the job description a couple of times before your job interview will give you certainty of what they're looking for. Pinpointing what they need will provide you with the necessary information to adapt your speech when engaging. You may direct your answers to fit as much as possible the requirements they're searching for. Leveraging the information from the job description can provide you with laser focus, further sparking interest in your profile.

3) Prepare for hard questions. By design, job interviews are supposed to be relatively challenging for the interviewee. Recruiters use this moment not only to assess you as a person but also discretely assess your skills relative to the open position. Some questions to prepare for may be "What are your weak points?," "What's your superpower?," "Why do you want to work for our company?," "Do you have Web3 experience?" Whatever they ask, your replies need to be swift and solid. Practicing with a friend before the interviews can even train your mind to spin the most tricky of questions too.

4) Master your backstory. We all have experience; we all have a past. As varied as they may be, you must tailor your backstory to the specific role you're enquiring for. In our context, you must promote an enhanced version of your Web3 experience, depending on how well versed in the industry you are. Leave out the unrelated segments of your personal and professional life until only the most apposite of your endeavors remain. Curating your backstory in such a manner will provide direction to the general conversation while further reinforcing your relevance to the opening.

5) Craft pertinent questions. Akin to the hiring process, preparing some smart questions beforehand can be a powerful tool during your interview. By asking two or three smart questions related to the company, role, services, technology, or methodology can automatically make you look like you possess the experience to fulfil the role. Questions such as "What's the company's main priority for this fiscal year?," "What KPIs are expected?," "What are the main challenges faced in this role?" can be used to show your attentiveness while providing you with some interesting insights of what might await you once hired.

6) Prepare your equipment. Make sure your computer doesn't need an update, your Internet is working, and you know which channel the interview will take place on, for example: Zoom, WhatsApp, phone call, Microsoft Teams, Google Meet, etc. Once informed, download the application of that tool and set it up correctly. Try a mock call with a close friend just

to make sure your audio is clear and video fluid. If you add a virtual background, keep it simple. Once you're sure everything works, log in to the waiting room of the meeting 20 minutes before the interview starts and double check. Doing this allows you the bandwidth to do a quick reboot or update if your computer requires it.

7) Prepare your environment. If your environment is buzzing with noise or visual pollution, it will be hard to create a comfortable environment for the recruiters and yourself. Firstly, make sure you're in a quiet, calm location with no background noise or interference. In other words, don't take your interview while in a café or a high street. Close all windows, doors, and potential openings where noise may enter. Secondly, prepare your background. If you have a nice natural setting, such as a tidy home office or room, this can be fine. If you have neither, it's preferable to adopt a virtual background and apply it on your communication tool. As one chooses their virtual background, sticking to a simple, elegant form will suffice. Don't choose a wacky, swashbuckling one as you may not come across as serious. Keep it simple. Finally, check and enhance your lighting so the recruiters may see you clearly without any shadows. The day of the interview, it's wise to double check all of the above around 20 minutes before your interview starts. This way if your light bulb burns out, your computer needs to update, or if another negative scenario occurs, you have some time to fix the problem. Once all is functional, on the day of your interview, be sure to:

8)   Be on time. Remember, this is your opportunity
     to shine. Don't take the risk of being stuck in
     your car because of traffic, for example. If you
     have other meetings, places to be, or other such
     imperatives, be sure to clear your schedule one
     hour before your interview starts and one hour after
     it's supposed to end. Reason being, you need to
     make sure you're on time with everything working
     and ready. Be sure to log in to your interview 3
     minutes before it's supposed to start. Depending
     on the communication tool, the organizer can
     see when you're waiting to be let in, and showing
     early presence is always good. If the interview goes
     extremely well, there's a chance you may also need
     to stay on for longer than expected. Make sure
     you have the bandwidth to do so by clearing your
     schedule a little more than required.

9)   Wardrobe. The way you will be dressed will also
     play an important role in the decision of the
     recruiters. In Web3, the vestimentary requirements
     are more lenient than in the traditional corporate
     environment, however, this doesn't mean that
     wearing a tank top or sunglasses will be in your
     favor. For men, a shirt or a basic, bland t-shirt can
     do the job just fine. For women, a colored T-shirt or
     a dress is fine too. However, you choose to dress, be
     sure to keep it relatively simple and not too much
     over the top. Web3 recruiters won't be impressed by
     your fashion sense, but more about your industry
     knowledge and experience.

10) Keep calm. Present yourself with a clear calm tone and don't overthink. Overthinking can lead to stress, creating the opposite effect we're looking for. The calmer you make yourself appear, the more confident and in control you'll appear. Working under pressure is normal in Web3, so you must show by your behavior that you're more than capable of handling it. Plus, you've prepared for this, so all will be fine; just sit back and show them what you're made out of!

11) Optimism. The second you enter the video conference, smile. Recruiters spend many hours on video conferences every single day, and the last thing they want is to hop on a call with someone negative. Beaming a big, great smile and speaking with an optimistic approach will bring the vibe of the call up and transform it into a warm, welcoming environment. On top of this, it will also create a much more open and free-flowing conversation between yourself and the recruiters. Creating this uplifting environment can increase your chances of getting hired, as your entire interview will be better received than and remembered than other applicants.

12) Show your true colors. Recruiters in Web3 aren't looking to hire robots, they're interested in hiring someone capable of bringing new value to the table, something the company doesn't already have. Being honest and showing them who you really are will be beneficial for both sides. Each and every one of us

has something truly unique about ourselves, this is one of the greatest strengths of humanity, diversity. A team of diverse individuals with the same goal will come up with multiple ways of achieving it; hence, diversity in individuals can be a great asset for companies. Plus, you can only hide your natural personal traits for so long, so if your personality isn't a match for a particular company, so be it. Better to move on and keep searching until you find a company in need of your person and unique traits. It's far more convalescing for the both of you in the long run.

13) Show interest. A good listener is hard to come by. As the majority of Web3 interviews take place over a video conference, you will be constantly watched by the recruiter. From experience, as one listens to an individual speaking over such a conference, the listener can really stand out by being a good listener. Pay attention to every word, nod your head in agreement, tilt your head to the side from time to time, and show the recruiter that you're listening through your actions. Keeping a coherent form of movement as the recruiter speaks will make them feel as if you definitely are listening, helping to further develop a positive relationship while fostering a friendly environment. All of these details will add up and give you an advantage over the competition. You may also ask some questions once they've finished speaking to really show them that you listened, understood, and are paying attention to details.

14) Demonstrate your competences. Take this opportunity to marry some of your skills or experiences with the information the recruiters will provide you with. Show them just how good a match you are for this role by making yourself not just seem relevant but also laying out examples of how you solved problems or challenges they're facing in the past. Don't just answer yes or no; take the time to explain. If you don't have an exact answer, that's fine, but try to point out how your skill set and experience will solve their current problems and challenges.

15) Take notes. Make sure you have a pen and paper by your side as you start the interview. Noting down important details such as the company challenges or what type of person they're looking to hire can equip you to tailor your replies accordingly. Also, you will need to write down the salary, commissions, and perks provided in case you need to negotiate one of them, any other relative information, and the next steps. Often, the recruiter will give you a time window for them to get back to you with their answer, knowing this will give you time to plan your follow-up without coming across too hasty.

As the interview comes to an end, there are a few things you can do to create a lasting impression while thanking them for their time:

16) Good manners. Ending on a high note is key to prolonging the lasting effect of your interview on the recruiters. Being polite and conversing in a polished manner can also score you some extra points. Even sending a thankful email the day after your interview will help you stand out from the crowd, and remind the recruiters that you're there. This simple gesture can really put you on a pedestal, heavily differentiating you from the other candidates.

17) Complete tasks early. Depending on the recruitment process, they may have given you a task to complete within a certain deadline. These tasks can range from an ethics exam, a proposal to enhance the sales team's performance all the way up to crafting a document on how you would tackle the current challenges. Don't procrastinate and leave them until the last minute. Be the early bird and finish way before the deadline. This will show your priorities to the recruiters, and you will be judged accordingly. Whatever they ask you to do, make sure it's perfect and delivered in a swift fashion.

18) Follow up. If they asked for some extra elements or credentials during the interview, make sure that you send them. Also, if you have asked for some more elements or credentials and haven't received them, don't be afraid to follow up via email. Asking for them again will promote your determination, plus remind them once again that you exist, keeping you at the top of their minds. Finally, ask for feedback; this is the only way you'll improve.

Summary

Web3 interviews can also be much more informal than your typical corporate ones. You can also leverage this opportunity to learn a bit more about the industry itself as you'll be researching the companies you have interviews with. Make the most out of every piece of information you can get your hands on, as it will help you build out a better picture of the wonderful world of Web3. Much like passing your driver's license, we don't all get it on the first go; the same may be said about your first interview in Web3. If you're not accepted on the first interview, it doesn't matter. Learn from each and every one to further develop your interview skills and deepen your industry knowledge. Always remember, if at first you don't succeed, try, try, and try again.

CHAPTER 5

Web3 Company Structures

Segment 1 – DAO

Unlike your average company in the more traditional lines of work and job opportunities, this upmost peculiar world of crypto once again doesn't follow the same set of rules. In any normal corporate job, seldom would you see on your contract that the company you've just joined is structured as some bizarre form of fiscal structure based in what may appear to be a fiscal paradise. If that was the case, it's more than likely that it would without a doubt raise more than one of your eyebrows. You would probably even raise that specific point in a carefully drafted email so as not to offend your new employers to the HR department asking for clarification on the intricacies of such a company structure. Here, in the world of Web3, unusual company structures and jurisdictions have actually become the norm for the majority of companies operating in this space. This isn't, however, by intention to create a shell company designed for money laundering in an offshore fiscal paradise, much like the company's involved in the Panama Papers scandal around 2016. Believe it or not, it's for the exact opposite reasons. Furthermore, the crypto industry has itself created new forms of company structures that some

© Alexander Rees-Evans 2024
A. Rees-Evans, *So You Want to Work in Crypto*,
https://doi.org/10.1007/979-8-8688-0503-5_5

governments just don't know how to grasp nor how to class them. When you start working in this beautiful industry and receive your first contract, you will most likely have questions and perhaps need some reassurance, especially if the company you'll be working for has a legal status you've never heard of before. In this chapter, we aim to shine a spotlight on these very complexities, starting with the DAO.

Of course, we lightly touched upon this acronym earlier on in the book, but when you're going to work full time under this umbrella, you'll without a doubt be glad that we did much more digging than just that. As of now, we're aware that DAO means Decentralized Autonomous Organization, but just what exactly does all of this mean and where did it come from?

Unlike what you may have imagined, the fundamental concept of a DAO has been around for quite some many years. In the 1960s (A Complete History of DAOs | Timeline 1960s to Now (cryptodose.net)), there was already hearsay about a fully functional yet decentralized protocol in some academic journals. You may even argue that a DAO is the ultimate form of democracy much craved by mankind for thousands of years. No human central form of power; all participants have a voice, and the results are binary without the possibility of corruption or fraud. Imagine if your government was run this way. Even if the DAO voted someone in, if that leader doesn't honor their word or starts to abuse power, that very same day, he or she could be voted out by the DAO and replaced in an instant. No voter fraud or fake ballets, no lying politicians, no shady business dealings, nor any wrongdoings. The entity put in place would permanently be at the mercy of the DAO.

The first time speaking of a DAO in crypto took place was in 2013 when Vitalik Buterin mentioned it in some of his writings (What is a decentralized autonomous organization, and how does a DAO work? (cointelegraph.com)). The first large-scale attempt to transform this ideological concept into a reality happened not long after, in 2016, when the former Ethereum protocol engineer Mr. Christoph Jentzsch released an open source code for an Ethereum-based investment platform, which turned out to be one of the most successful crowdfunding raises of all time. Over $150 million USD of public funding was raised in hopes of bringing this idea to life. Even by today's standards, that's an exceptional raise for even the largest of projects in Web3, even in a full-on Bull run. The goal of this raise was to power a community-driven blockchain fundraising structure known as "The DAO." Although the raise was by far a great success, not long after a major problem occurred that ultimately led The DAO to its demise. A hacker or group of hackers were able to find a vulnerability in the code and started using it to their advantage. Due to this exposure, over $60 million USD worth of Ethereum was stolen (about 14% of all Ethereum in circulation at that time), and the project slowly but surely started to slumber into the depths of the River Styx from Greek mythology.

You guessed it, a DAO really is the ultimate utopia of decentralization, but like always, it's not perfect. On top of technical vulnerabilities, there can also be centralization concerns too. Generally speaking, the way a modern DAO works is that you have to purchase the native tokens of the DAO and then stake them for a certain period of time to fully participate in the ecosystem. Depending on how the DAO is designed, voting periods or other decisions in the ecosystem can be skewed, as it's not rare that the more tokens you own and stake, the more weight you have in the process. In short, if you wish to heavily influence a DAOs decision and have deep pockets, all you need to do is buy a large portion of the DAOs native tokens and stake them. Today, some DAOs have taken this into consideration and only grant a certain amount of weight per vote, regardless of how many of their native tokens you may have bought to help equalize the playing field.

Another very interesting use for a DAO that could even affect you directly is not just the possibility for the DAO to vote on small issues, but very large issues such as hiring. This is exactly the case of the Telos blockchain when their DAO voted in Mr. Lee Erswell as the new CEO. Yes, you just read that correctly: a DAO made the decision on someone's future job and career path.

One more interesting example is that there are still Web3 crowdfunding platforms structured as DAOs, such as MarsDAO, where the employees are hired by c-levels, but all projects chosen for investment must be validated by a vote from the DAO prior to activating the fundraising mechanism.

In hindsight, you could almost compare DAO members to shareholders in a company. Today in the corporate world, we often hear that some find it outrageous that companies put the shareholders' interests before those of the employees of that very same company. We also hear that when the CEO of a company is underperforming, the shareholders want to replace them. In the corporate world, this decisive power is often among the largest handful of shareholders and the board of executives. In other words, the entities that invested a tremendous amount of money in exchange of company shares and the top c-levels and members. One of the main differences here the modern crypto DAOs seek to change is exactly that issue, the centralization of power and influence.

For example, in our scenario of the corporate world with shareholders, it's most likely that the most influential entities in the board meeting will be able to sway others to vote their way. Just as it's possible for the CEO whose job is on the line to try and corrupt the majority by promising to fire 2% of the global staff to pay our more dividends or whatever's in his power to bribe them with. One more big problem in this model is that only a select few actually have the possibility to voice their concerns and have weight in decisions. The average Joe who bought $150 USD worth of their shares a year and a half ago will never in a million years be granted any form of voicing their opinion on this matter. And that goes for the other hundreds of thousands, if not millions, of minority shareholders of that company's stock.

The modern crypto DAOs try to even out this decisive power among all shareholders, no matter how big or how small that person's stock is. In short, DAOs are a much fairer form of the shareholder concept in the traditional financial markets. They have the goal of providing equal weight in all decisions from every token holder. As we agreed, not all DAOs are perfect, but they're striving towards that end goal of decentralization of decision-making. Not only is this ethically positive, it also happens to be an amazing way to enable your community to be much more than just a stakeholder; they can actually participate in shaping the future of that very project through the unified force of the DAO. Often, the DAO is structured in such a way that individuals in the DAO can't simply raise questions and topics out of thin air to vote upon, but it's your company that determines them. Once your company executives have to decide on a question, they will then refer that question to the DAO. Once the DAO has voted and voiced their collective opinion, whatever they decide is final, and your company will have to execute accordingly.

Now not all Web3 companies are DAOs, but they are becoming more and more common. It may very well be that you apply for a job in Web3 without even realizing, they have a DAO in place! If you're not fully aware of the general concept of that DAO, you may have quite a surprise on your first day at work. If you do end up working under one of these structures, be sure to ask the implications, dates, and subjects on what the DAO will be voting on beforehand. Don't be shy to ask even the hardest of questions, such as "To what extent can the DAO influence our workload, positions or company health?". These aren't taboo questions, as you not only have the right to know, but you must. As an employee under their umbrella, you must know what that implies for the company and for yourself.

Segment 2 – Fiscal Domiciles

Aside from that special DAO structure, the other major component we mentioned at the beginning of this chapter was the fiscal domicile of the company itself. In the majority of cases, when you receive your work contract, you won't find a classical US- or UK-registered company as you could imagine. For the reasons we stated above, the classical countries just haven't been able to keep up with the fast-moving pace of this industry.

It so happens that the majority of these smaller offshore countries, such as Bermuda, the Cayman Islands, and Dubai, for example, have actually laid out very clear laws and regulations for crypto companies, unlike the more powerful countries. It goes without saying that there are some fiscal advantages too, but the main reason why crypto companies are calling these places their fiscal domiciles is because you can create the appropriate company structures and operate legally. As of today, the majority of the "old world" hasn't been able to pivot nor create a transparent or friendly enough environment for crypto companies to flourish. As a matter of fact, you don't even have to go to the other side of the world, Estonia and Latvia, among other eastern European countries, have also created very welcoming and transparent crypto regulations, so it's not uncommon to find that your company may be structured there. It is, however, important for you to understand what's happening on a fiscal and legal level so that when you sign your contract, you're aware of how your company is or isn't aligning itself to operate legally.

With the likes of the SEC, MICA, and other regulatory entities starting to tighten their grip on the Web3 industry, others are embracing this change and even have programs or grants in place to assist growth in this sector. To reassure you on what you may find on your contract, we're now going to explore some of the usual fiscal domiciles for Web3 companies and their characteristics:

1) Zug (Switzerland)

   Regulatory environment: As always, Switzerland manages to always place itself as a friendly hub for financial activities, but in our case, it's especially Zug that has taken the limelight for the crypto space regulatory environment. For a while now, Zug has created a meticulous and transparent framework, providing a heavily monitored, but clear path for all crypto companies to take even if they're starting to implement harsher regulations for stablecoins. The Swiss Financial Market Supervision Authority (FINMA) is the regulatory entity charged with enforcing their crypto regulation.

Infrastructure: Commonly known as the "Crypto Valley," you can easily find a vibrant panache of blockchain start-ups, accelerators, legal firms, and venture capitalists by the dozen. Although there has been an unfortunate collapse in recent times with the bankruptcy of Signature Bank, many other crypto and crypto-friendly banks flourish in the environment of Zug.

Tax benefits: It goes without saying that Switzerland is indeed well known for having very low taxes, and Zug has one of the lowest in the country. Due to their clear regulations, they have also created beneficial tax rulings designed only for crypto companies regarding VAT and capital gains.

Legal framework: Thanks to their understanding of the Web3 industry, they have not only been able to create clear definitions of crypto-assets but have even crafted specific guidance on KYC/AML requirements, among other unique crypto activities such as IEOs.

Government support: On top of openly supporting cryptocurrencies and blockchain technologies, the government has encouraged the formation of associations such as the Swiss Blockchain Association or the Crypto Valley Association, helping further promote and evolve the industry.

The government also put in place the "Blockchain Act" to provide an analog form of guidance to all that wish to structure themselves on their grounds. Finally, the government often seeks consultancy from industry stakeholders and experts to help them constantly improve the environment already in place.

2) Dubai (UAE)

Regulatory environment: Since recent years, Dubai has placed itself at the forefront of the blockchain space. Spearheaded by the Dubai Financial Services Authority (DFSA) and the Dubai Multi Commodities Center (DMCC), a clear regulatory framework has been put in place, alongside golden visas to attract global talent, not only for the blockchain space.

Infrastructure: Dubai has an outstanding infrastructure, with entire towns dedicated to specific forms of business. Also, Dubai is a global hub for ultra-high net worth and high net worth individuals, making it one of the best places in the world for networking. Additionally, they have very accessible airports and host some of the most infamous crypto events in the world, such as Token 2049. Their constantly booming economy and desire to embrace blockchain technologies makes Dubai one of the best crypto infrastructures globally.

Tax benefits: Although Dubai is a relatively expensive place to be based, they do, however, offer a most favorable tax regime including zero corporate tax and no income tax among many other fiscal advantages.

Legal framework: The DFSA and the DMCC are the main policy and regulatory authorities for the blockchain space. There is also the Dubai Blockchain Center helping provide real industry insight to these authorities, assisting them to make much more strategic decisions that are beneficial not only for the country but will keep the industry happy too.

Supportive government: Dubai's rulers and blockchain related entities have openly embraced this technology to such a degree that they have spawned the idea of becoming the world's first ever blockchain powered government (Dubai Blockchain Strategy | Blockchain Dubai | Digital Dubai). Needless to say, they already host some of the world's largest crypto events and have one of the most efficient crypto regulations available today.

3) Bermuda

Regulatory environment: You may not have known this, but Bermuda is one of the most forward-thinking countries in this space. An exceptionally clear regulation for digital assets has been put in place thanks to the Bermuda Monetary Authority (BMA) helping put together the Digital Asset Business Act (DABA), solidifying the rules.

Infrastructure: As the majority of the GDP of Bermuda comes from the financial industry, and more specifically the insurance sector, they already had one of the best infrastructures to start with. Furthermore, they also happen to have the fourth largest GDP per capita in the modern world, making

Bermuda not only one of the most stable but one of the richest countries in the world. With their steady politics and immense wealth, they can keep strategically investing in this industry for years to come without any major shifts due to elections.

Tax benefits: Bermuda's tax regime is one of the most favorable in the world, thanks to no corporate income tax, no capital gains tax, nor VAT. This country is one of the most tax friendly in the modern world.

Legal framework: The DABA provides a very robust and comprehensive legal framework for any crypto company looking to set up shop in Bermuda, destined to ensure regulatory clarity while also keeping investor's protection at heart.

Supportive government: The Bermudan government is probably one of the most physically active governments in the entire space. At certain large crypto events, such as Consensus in Austin Texas, you may even see the Premier of their country, Mr. David Burt, walking around the conference with the company of his fellow ambassadors, such as Anthony J Howell, and openly engaging with individuals. They have also tasked the Bermuda Development Agency (BDA) to organize fabulous side events where invited individuals can discuss in person with Beermuda's high-ranking individuals their ideas on policy and general consensus of the blockchain space. They are by far one of the most supportive countries of blockchain technology in the world, proven by their physical presence and policy decisions.

4) Estonia

Regulatory environment: You may have been thinking to yourself that all of the crypto-friendly jurisdictions are located far from Europe, but there's still a small handful of crypto-friendly countries in Europe itself. Estonia is one of the best domiciles for CEXs and wallet providers, as the Financial Intelligence Unit (FUI) heading up the crypto regulations for the country has laid out a progressive, inexpensive, and clear set of regulations and licensing for crypto ventures.

Infrastructure: It may not be as shiny as Dubai, but everything needed to operate a crypto business is there. To further encourage working in this space, the government has created the e-residency program, enabling applicants the possibility to work from Estonia without having to apply for a regular visa.

Tax benefits: Estonia boasts a rather cordial tax environment too, including a simplified flat tax system for corporate tax and zero tax on retained earnings compared to its much more aggressive European neighbors.

Legal framework: Estonia hasn't just tasked the FUI with the immense task of structuring the corporate side of things; they also have put strict verification levels in place, starting with stringent Anti-Money Laundering (AML) and Counter Terrorist Financing (CTF) checks on a regular basis.

Supportive government: Estonia is highly supportive of blockchain technologies as a whole and likes to promote itself as a leader in this digital space. On top of their e-residency program, Estonia isn't against the idea of speaking with industry leaders to provide them with valuable insight that can influence some of their decisions in policy. Finally, they have created a sandbox-like approach with much lighter regulations for start-ups looking to commence building their product.

5)   Cayman Islands

Regulatory environment: The Cayman Islands have adapted to this modern era exceptionally well. Originally criticized for being a fiscal paradise, today they have proven to the world that they're capable of implementing very clear and strict regulations when needed. With the Cayman Islands Monetary Authority overviewing everything blockchain, they made their regulations official by enacting the Virtual Assets Service Providers (VASP) Act, serving as guidelines for all who wish to structure their company on these shores.

Infrastructure: Much like Bermuda, the Cayman Islands have a significant history of dealing in the traditional financial sector, providing them with a great foundation to participate in the blockchain space. Unlike what you may have originally thought, the Cayman Islands have a very strong legal and regulatory system, which is why a lot of traditional hedge funds are domiciled over there too, making it a very solid and reassuring environment for many crypto companies.

Tax benefits: Of course, there are obvious tax benefits that come with being domiciled in the Cayman Islands. The main ones are zero corporate tax and zero income tax as the same may be said about capital gains tax. Once again, it's arguably one of the most preferential tax systems in the world.

Legal framework: The Cayman Islands decided to keep everything extremely straightforward for their framework in regard to crypto companies. All is neatly stipulated and organized in the VASP Act, explaining in great detail their crypto regulations.

Supportive government: The Cayman Islands are indeed highly supportive of the crypto industry as a whole. Although they aren't as physically involved as Bermuda, their government constantly strives to be on top of any new requirements for the regulation of digital assets. The Cayman Enterprise City (CEC) is a special economic zone put in place by the government, offering even more benefits and incentives for tech and blockchain companies alike. The CIMA and government also engage on a regular basis with important industry leaders to help them further shape and enhance their current blockchain regulations.

6)   Saudi Arabia

Regulatory environment: Saudi Arabia may have taken a little bit more time to fully engage in the blockchain space, but since it has, it's become by far one of the most influential and promising lands to set up a crypto company in the near future. With many unique initiatives led by the Saudi Arabian Monetary Authority (SAMA) and the Capital

Market Authority (CMA), today they are constantly improving the foundations for one of the most efficient and clear forms of regulations possible for blockchain companies.

Infrastructure: Much like Duabi, Saudi Arabia has invested heavily in their infrastructure for quite some years now. Furthermore, they're by far one of the wealthiest countries in the world and will most likely invest phenomenal amounts of money in this sector as it further evolves. They've only just got started and we're sure to see them become even more dominant in this industry over the next few years.

Tax benefits: Their tax regime is also quite welcoming too with exceptional tax benefits for all businesses plus low corporate tax and various incentives for foreign investments.

Legal framework: The full spectrum of regulation may not be fully completed as of Q2 2024 but will soon be. The advantage of laying down the foundations now enables Saudi Arabia to create fresh regulations and learn from the mistakes of others. Their regulation is expected to be one of the best in the world upon full completion.

Supportive government: Now cryptocurrencies are neither legal or illegal as of today's regulatory environment, yet Saudi Arabia's stance on blockchain technology and derivatives is extremely positive. By 2030, they aim to invest massively in emerging sectors, including blockchain technology, Fintech, and even Central Bank Digital Currencies (CBDCs).

There are of course many other crypto-friendly countries, such as Liechtenstein, Singapore, and Hong Kong, among many more, but the ones illustrated above are the most predominantly used for setting up crypto companies and/or have incredible potential in the upcoming years. The goal of sharing these rather high-level details is because you will most definitely receive a working contract from a company based in one of the above. If you're not aware of these company and regulatory intricacies, you may be surprised when presented with such a contract. The reason for sharing this additional information with you is to not only reassure you when you do receive a contract mentioning one of these lands, but also to provide you with the reasoning behind it so you understand why the company you'll work for has set themselves up in such a fashion.

Segment 3 – Levels of Crypto Start-Ups

As you now know, companies in the crypto realm have very different thought processes and challenges compared to their analog twins. One of the main challenges you'll face when applying for a job in this industry is making sure the company is viable. In short, the larger and more established the company, usually the more funds they have, hence a longer or shorter runway. On the other hand, the larger, more established Web3 companies have higher requirements when they hire staff, such as experience in the industry. This isn't to say that it's not possible to join one of these industry titans for a first job; it's just very unlikely. The plethora of company levels in this sector really is quite astonishing, and this one of the reasons why the job opportunities are plentiful. Not only this, but there really is tremendous opportunity to accumulate great wealth in just a few years if you get on the right train at the right moment. In this segment, we'll explore the levels of different companies in this industry alongside their pros and cons.

Above, we touched upon three main parameters you need to consider when applying for a job in this industry: Viability, Attainability, and the rewards.

Viability directly translates to how sustainable the company itself is. As this is a world of start-ups, the number of companies that don't make it through Bear markets due to a lack of funding is quite astonishing. Any company that's spent over four years in this industry is considered a veteran to some extent, which we can all agree isn't really the case in the traditional corporate world. The capacity of the company you'll be working for to survive without any revenue over a period of time is referred to as their runway. Just like a plane taking off from a runway in an airport, the runway's mathematically designed to provide enough length for the plane to build up speed and take to the air. If the runway is too short, however, the plane won't have sufficient room, won't build up enough speed to take off, and will end up crashing into the fence at the end of it. Just like the runways for planes have more than enough meters in length for the plane to accelerate and reach the speed necessary until it takes off, companies are the same. In our case, a company's runway can be increased by adding more funds to the bank. On average, companies try to have a minimum of one year of spare funds they can use to keep the company running until the market picks up and clients start purchasing their services or products again.

Attainability in the context used above describes just how tangible it is for you to acquire a certain job in a company. For example, if you apply to be the head of marketing of a crypto PR firm but have little to no experience in that position, it's highly unlikely you'll get the job. To add insult to injury, if you apply for that same job at one of the most reputable crypto PR firms in the industry, it will be even less likely. On the other hand, if you are qualified in that domain, have some experience of a similar position in the traditional corporate world, and apply to be head of marketing in a small, relatively new crypto PR firm, your chances of obtaining the position in that given company are all of a sudden much higher. It's all about being realistic, and even if you think you're capable of performing in a certain position in a reputable crypto company, try to aim just below. This isn't about reaching for the stars and getting your dream job on the first try; it's about getting your foot through the door, adjusting to the industry pace, understanding the blockchain industry, then strategically navigating through it until you're eligible for your dream job.

Rewards for your efforts can be quite exceptional in this industry, as we observed in the earlier pages of this book. Due to the opportunistic and speculative nature of the Web3 industry, there are real possibilities for companies to generate exceptional wealth. This isn't just on the side of salaries, but more so on the side of dividends, company shares, or tokens. A lot of the companies in Web3 have or plan to have their own native tokens. Think Ethereum or even BNB; both of these tokens have increased tremendously in their dollar value since their release. If you were able to join one of these companies before the release of their native tokens, the chances are you would have been granted a portion of the total token supply that would easily be worth a few million dollars in today's market. However, to obtain this type of reward, you need to get into a very early stage company that may not even be well funded. As the salaries in those companies are generally low, they promise tremendous compensation for sticking with them through the hard times once and if they're able to launch a successful token. Another option for companies is to hit an IPO in Nasdaq or other large public exchanges. Crypto companies with the desire to do this usually design their financial plan, runway, and strategy from inception with this in mind. This isn't necessarily a bad thing either; it just means that they may want to keep expenses low, sell their company shares and exit, or simply change company direction afterwards. If you join one of these companies, much like the promise of high-value tokens in our previous case, you'll likely not have a consequent salary but a portion of company shares to make it worth your while. Compared to a company without this strategy at their core, other companies will be designed to do one thing and one thing only, generate turnover. There won't be any immediate launch of a token potentially worth millions of dollars, nor will there be the prestige of hitting an IPO at Nasdaq, but you'll more than likely earn serious money every month.

Now that we've discussed the three pillars of decision making for jobs, let's dive a little more into the actual levels of companies in order to provide you with some more insight on what to look out for:

1. Idea stage

    Characteristics: At this first stage of development, the startup is usually composed of only a handful of individuals, mostly all working part time with a heavy focus on refining their vision. Generally speaking, they're finalizing the Whitepaper, business model, market research, and if they have some funds, building the first version of their product/ service.

    Priorities:

    – Concept development

    – Market research

    – Whitepaper

    – Building the core team

    Funding: Typically speaking, they're bootstrapped with little to no funds or are supported by their own funds or those of friends and family.

2. Pre-seed stage

    Characteristics: The company has set up a legal entity and is generally building their Minimum Viable Product (MVP) and fine-tuning their business models and tokenomics if they plan to have a token.

They now aim to start raising funds to continue development and hire some more team members to help accelerate their growth.

Priorities:

– Develop an MVP

– Expand the core team

– Initial market fit validation

– Community building

– Fundraising

Funding: The majority of projects in the pre-seed stage have secured some funds from friends, family, and/or angel investors.

3. Seed stage

Characteristics: By this stage, the company is expected to have a working MVP, have successfully completed the fundraise of their seed round plus focus heavily on marketing and client/community acquisition. Now with a slightly larger team and some funds, the company should start gaining traction.

Priorities:

– Product/service development

– User/client feedback and tweaking of the product/service accordingly

– Building market presence

– Scaling the team

– Fundraising

Funding: In this round, the company has sufficient funds to start paying out salaries to all of the team members and even scale some more. They should have funds from venture capitalists and angel investors at this stage without forgetting that once this round is completed, they may have a quick Key Opinion Leader (KOL) and private round before they go public. These last three small rounds can happen relatively quickly through launchpads or IEO/IDOs.

4.   Series A

Characteristics: Considering the company accomplished the KOL, private, and public rounds, the next round is the infamous series A. This generally means that the company has significant traction, some time in the market, and is scaling their products/services and customers/community. This doesn't, however, mean that they're well funded, as opening a series A round can indicate that the company has little to no runway left and needs to raise more funds to survive.

Priorities:

– Scaling of products/services

– Scaling of customers/community

– Marketing

– Hire expensive talent

– Develop strong strategic partnerships

Funding: Funding from all of the previous investors, but now they target large venture capital firms, hedge funds, and large corporate investors, as they'll be raising significant amounts of funds.

5.   Series B

Characteristics: The company has significant traction is well implemented in the industry with a very large team. The business model is validated, and now they put all efforts into obtaining a larger market share.

Priorities:

– Expanding into new markets

– Enhancing product/service features and user/customer experience

– Scaling of their marketing and sales team

– Increasing operational efficiency

– Finding strategic investors

Funding: On top of all of the previous investors mentioned having already injected funds into the company earlier on, this round really focuses on tier 1 venture capitalists, private equity, family offices, fiduciaries, and hedge funds to invest.

Nelson Mandela once said that education is the most powerful weapon on earth, by educating you on the different types, levels, and structures of companies in this industry. You will by far be equipped with enough knowledge to understand what the general consensus and goals of crypto companies are. A key note here is that depending on how the company's structured, where it's domiciled, and all of the other intricacies we discussed will provide you valuable insight as to if that company is a right fit for you and aligned with your goals and expectations. Combining that information with the three pillars of decision-making when accepting or declining a job offer in a crypto company, you have all the information needed to make wise strategic decisions when entering the crypto workforce.

CHAPTER 6

Web3 Working Environment

A big industry secret often swept under the rug by the crypto industry is the notion of "wartime" vs. "peacetime" companies coupled with the ability to adapt swiftly. Once employed in the crypto industry, this takes on a distinct and stark reality that you need to be prepared for. Unlike the traditional corporate world where tech giants like Google epitomize the stability and growth of "peacetime" companies, their crypto counterparts inherently operate in a constant "wartime" state. This unique environment shapes every aspect of working in Web3, from leadership styles to daily operations and employee experiences. In the crypto sector, "wartime" isn't just a phase; it's the norm. Companies are perpetually navigating through a landscape rife with volatility, regulatory uncertainty, technological disruptions, and fierce competition. This environment necessitates a continual state of vigilance, quick decision-making, and adaptability.

As you're researching potential job positions in crypto, be sure to keep in mind that there are many different types of CEOs and company traits, which we will explore in this chapter. Imagine working for Vitalik Buterin, from a young basement gamer to the founder of a billion dollar company. A lot of founders in this industry made tremendous money overnight and don't necessarily have great people skills as you would usually see from a CEO in the corporate world. Depending on the CEO style and company

© Alexander Rees-Evans 2024
A. Rees-Evans, *So You Want to Work in Crypto*,
https://doi.org/10.1007/979-8-8688-0503-5_6

culture, values, ethos, and vision, your experience working in Web3 will differ heavily. Armed with all of this information, leverage it to help you make the best possible decisions when confronted with choices!

Before we further explore the subtleties of this, we need to first take a step back and understand what "peacetime" and "wartime" companies are and how they work.

We will begin by exploring the role and personality traits of CEOs.

An understanding of the distinction between "peacetime" and "wartime" characteristics starts with the CEO of the company. Being captains of their ship, they and they alone dictate the company rhythm and culture of the venture. Heavily pressured by shareholders, investors, competition, regulations, and market conditions, they have very different day-to-day tasks when compared with other employees and C-level executives. For example, the CFO and other C-level executives generally imitate the company management styles set by the CEO, which dictates the flow and company direction. However, as there are often different periods in a company's lifespan, CEOs are often replaced following a major change in the company. The new CEO often has very different personality traits when compared with his predecessor Such changes in CEOs are much more common in the traditional corporate world, as the founder usually takes a large step back once the company's successful. In this industry, interestingly enough the founders usually stay in a very controlling position rather than one of oversight as we can see with Justin Sun, the founder of Tron, and Vitalik Buterin from Ethereum.

We will now explore different types of CEOs.

"The Entrepreneur"

The entrepreneur-style CEO is often behind the very idea of that company. They love to build companies from the ground up by hiring the initial team members, transforming the idea into a functioning company, and then creating a reasonably sized portfolio of clients. Once the company is fully functional, they optimize cash flow by keeping employee numbers and company expenses to a minimum and focus on growing the company's immediate valuation. Once they're happy with the valuation, the next step is to sell the company and make their "exit." This is a very unique type of CEO, as they seldom head up large firms for long periods of time and don't have a long-term goal benefiting the company, only themselves and other shareholders. After each exit, they search for another venture they can build up and sell off a few years later again; it's always a start-and-repeat process. In the crypto realm, it's not uncommon to come across this type of CEO, as there's always potential for fast turnover here. If you do happen to be in a company run by such a CEO, keep in mind your current position is probably not a lifelong, one but you can, however, negotiate company shares that you can also sell as the company's being acquired, potentially giving you years of financial freedom before you need to work again.

"The Flashy Boss"

Now this type of CEO loves to dress well, has a fancy car, and will always take the employees and clients out for lunch or to high-end bars. They're the same person that will have a limited edition bag of TaylorMade golf clubs but couldn't get a par five to save the company. As you guessed, this is the cash splasher and the great deal maker! Constantly spending but also creating phenomenal partnerships, promoting tremendous company growth and revenue. Usually, such CEOs are appointed in very successful companies in times of market peaks when cash is plentiful and the company is thriving. The goal of having this particular governor is to keep the company at the top and spend whatever is needed to remain there. May it be by flying first class to conferences around the world or even organizing the most lavish of side events to impress their surroundings, they mean big business and aren't afraid to show it.

"The Conservative Dictator"

In times of low cash flow, bad market conditions or even very strong regulatory pressure, you'll often find a very different style of CEO at the helm. Here, it's all about limiting expenses by any means necessary while keeping the company 100% operational. Think of it as the emergency mode your own body can activate if you're cold. Slowly, your heartbeat decreases, blood stops flowing to your extremities, and your body focuses only on keeping your main organs functional. In the crypto/corporate world, it means times are bad and the only focus is to do whatever is necessary in order to keep the company alive. This may mean ceasing activities or services that don't produce positive cash flow, letting go of company employees and/or branches, or even renegotiating salaries with the remaining employees. This CEO isn't in a position to make friends; their only goal and objective is to keep the company functioning until market conditions improve or positive cash flow is strong again.

The above examples are just some of the many, and prior to taking a deep dive into the Peacetime CEO and the Wartime CEO, we first need to understand what exactly are peacetime and wartime companies.

Wartime Companies

What a lot of people don't realize is the actual category of all of the companies in this industry – they're Wartime companies, not peacetime. Ben and Andreessen Horowitz define this perfectly, "Wartime companies are fending off an existential threat." This means that there's so much external and internal pressure on the company's survival that they're in a constant battle to stay alive. Due to the amount of competition between companies and constantly changing regulations, your competitors can take the edge, hence your clients. This is the reason why a lot of the CEOs of Web3 companies are very demanding, don't tolerate excuses, and swear often. There's nothing quite comparable to waking up at 07h00mins in the morning and being embarrassed in front of 50 people on a live Zoom call. If it happens and you get treated unfairly at brief moments, don't take it personally; it happens to everyone at some point. Listen as to why you're receiving this criticism, then rectify your actions to get back on track.

Peacetime Companies

In the normal Web2 world, especially Fortune 500s and large corporations, the CEOs and general management style is what we call "Peacetime." A Peacetime company is the exact opposite of a Wartime company. Peacetime companies are not under any existential threat and are in good financial shape with a very big and bright future. A classic example of a Peacetime company is Google. They have free employee salad and fruit bars, free juicy smoothies, meditation rooms, and ping pong tables. Every employee is relaxed, can take time off on vacation, have naps in between some meetings, and is even encouraged to be creative and start their own side projects. The C-levels are moving around the office on electric scooters and high-fiving team members for the great morning brainstorming session; you get the picture.

Examples: Shift from "Peacetime" to "Wartime"

A great example of a big Web 2 company shifting from Peacetime to Wartime recently is X (formally known as Twitter). Originally owned by Jack Dorsey, the kind of chilled hippie figure sitting on billions of dollars, it mirrored the same culture for all of the Twitter employees. They had big paychecks, only a couple of meetings per day, and could really enjoy the company perks such as food bars, sports rooms, yoga courses, etc. We've probably all seen at least one or two videos of high-level employees from Twitter posting TikToks while at work, showing off the new meditation and cry rooms they got installed so they could unwind from their stressful days of work. Once Elon Musk took over, he completely switched the company culture and management style from a Peacetime, to a Wartime company environment. By simply stating that people would have to work harder and stop playing ping pong during company hours, the majority of the company employees were livid! They weren't taking any of this, hence some of them ended up losing their jobs while the rest actually had to work.

The final example to provide a full view of the common mindset In the Web3 industry is Netflix. Before they became big, they were actually struggling a lot and had a big monthly burn rate for salaries. The CEO Reed Hastings was facing a huge dilemma as he didn't really have any bad employees; some were good and some were excellent. He made the decision to fire all of the good employees and keep only the excellent ones. He thought he would get a huge backlash from the left-over team members and they'd all just quit; to his surprise, they didn't. With a much smaller yet efficient team, they actually increased productivity immensely, superseding greatly their prior productivity obtained with a much larger team! The difference is that the remaining employees actually wanted the company to become great, and once the team was downsized, leaving only the high performers, they were free to unleash their full potential without any interruptions from the people who just liked their normal 9-to-5 job.

In Web3, this is the general culture, Wartime companies only keep their top performers, regardless of your role or position. They're often referred to as "A players," meaning that they're star performers. Because of this refined team quality, it's quite usual for the individual team members to be left by themselves, as they're productive with nobody on their backs. This doesn't mean, however that their performance isn't tracked and monitored. It simply grants top employees the ability to fulfil their duties and make certain decisions without having to wait for C-level approval.

Another interesting phrase in the industry is the "Critical hit." This is often compared to how big cats save their energy for that one big kill. They don't make fifty small attempts, each one slowly sapping their energy to the state that they have nothing left in their tanks, then die of hunger. They calculate the risks, time, and energy involved in taking down a prey and its Return On Investment (ROI). In the Web3 world, you often have Key Performance Indicator (KPIs). Your KPIs determine if you've hit the target given to you in your respective role. For example, if you're a developer, it may be finishing the new backend within 25 days; if you're hired as the new Chief Operations Officer (COO), it may be to increase Customer Relationship Management (CRM) activity by 10% within 20 days; an account or sales manager may close a deal for a minimum of $30,000 USDT within your first month. The KPIs heavily vary depending on the role you have, but everyone has them. Your critical hit is usually tangent to your KPIs when you start. It's the one big KPI you need to hit to stay onboard.

Now that we have a deeper understanding of the differences and nuances between peacetime and wartime companies, we can add our two final CEO styles to the list.

"Peacetime CEO"

The company's finances are extremely solid, the competition is lacking, and the future is very bright. This CEO will provide generous pay checks, great company healthcare, and office facilities. A job position in such a company is relatively secure; hence, you may focus on building a lifelong career within this one entity. Sometimes, you can even be encouraged to start your own creative side projects while you still work full time! The CEO is here to gently keep the company on track and develop tremendous public trust and long-term acquisitions.

"Wartime CEO"

The company's constantly under existential threat. There's no focus on long-term goals, and every day each employee must give 100% in their respective role. The CEO must keep pushing every single person to do their best and will not hesitate to fire on the spot and find a replacement the next day. Due to the real possibility of the company filing for bankruptcy, employees generally don't focus on building a lifelong career and focus more on completing their tasks by the book. No time for credibility but big chances for rewards as the CEO needs to keep only A players so doesn't hesitate to provide big paychecks and company shares or tokens. This CEO is positioned to keep the company alive and overcome constant competition and threats.

In the realm of crypto, the topic of salaries is as dynamic and mysterious as the industry itself. Due to it being an incredibly young industry, the lack of qualified and devoted talent is rife. If you're able to build and equip yourself with relevant experience, a deep Web3 network and a tremendous work ethic, you'll soon find yourself being worth more than gold to a crypto recruiter! Within this spectrum of employee value, resides a quiet, discreet chart of crypto compensation, where the promise of lucrative rewards is often balanced by the experience and work ethic you bring to the table.

In the crypto industry, salaries can range widely, often reflecting the volatile nature of the sector. Unlike traditional jobs, where paychecks are relatively predictable, crypto compensation can fluctuate dramatically based on several factors – market conditions, company performance, and individual role results. And even what part of the world you live in. The following will elaborate upon the types of salaries of which different levels of employees can receive. Please keep in mind that the following salary guidelines are based for employees living in Europe, Asia, and the United States. Employees from the Middle East should expect a little more, employees from India should expect to halve them, and employees from certain African countries should divide them by three. These salary discrepancies between country/continent of residency exist to purely help match the individual's cost of living. In short, your salary rises or decreases to a certain degree based on the cost of living in your area. The following examples should help bring further clarity and depth to the salaries of an employee in Web3:

> Entry-level positions: For those just stepping into the crypto world, the starting salaries can be modest yet promising. Roles like account managers, sales representatives, or junior developers might see figures ranging from $1,000 to $4,000 per month. Another salary component often included in your contract are the additional perks. These can be composed of company shares, tokens, and commissions that can significantly boost overall compensation.

> Mid-level expertise: With one or two years of working in Web3 under your belt, the earning potential in crypto starts to rise significantly. Salaries for positions requiring specialized knowledge or a proven track record in the industry, such as business developers or experienced marketers, can receive anywhere from $3,000 to $6,000 per month. Again, this base salary is often supplemented with performance-based bonuses or equity in the company, making the total package even more attractive.

Senior roles: For the veterans, the seasoned experts who've navigated the highs and lows of the crypto world, salaries can soar. We're talking about figures that range from $10,000 to over $100,000 per month. These are the trailblazers, the innovators, and the top strategists whose deep industry knowledge and extensive networks command top dollar. The compensation packages at this level often include substantial equity stakes or token allocations, reflecting the value these individuals bring to the table.

You must also take into consideration the unique aspects of working in crypto, including the inherent volatility of the industry, as this extends to salaries as well. A booming market can mean windfall gains, but the reverse is also true. Companies might offer generous token allocations or equity as part of compensation packages, but the actual value of these can fluctuate wildly with market conditions. It's capital to negotiate your base salary, commissions, company shares, or token allocations based on the possibility of these perks actually becoming valuable. For example, if your company provides you shares and they plan to list on NASDAQ, don't be afraid to ask when and even if the company's on track for this. This is where the high-risk, high-reward nature of the crypto industry becomes evident. On the one hand, you have the potential for astronomical gains if the company's token value skyrockets or if it hits a major exchange. On the other hand, there's the sobering reality that a market downturn or a project's failure could see those values plummet. Think wisely when negotiating your contract; is it better to have a larger base salary or more shares of the company?

Adding to the never-ending uniqueness of working in the crypto industry, many crypto companies offer salaries in cryptocurrencies like USDT (Tether), directly transferring funds to employees' digital wallets.

This method underscores the industry's digital native ethos and offers a level of convenience and immediacy. However, it also introduces a new layer of responsibility and competency for employees. It's heavily recommended to create an account on a large CEX such as Binance so you may actually and directly switch your crypto into fiat currency such as EUR or USD, so you may then transfer the fiat funds straight to your bank account. Be sure to pre-open this account and pass Know Your Customer (KYC) beforehand so once you receive your first pay, you can simply do the transfers immediately.

I would like to take a second here and develop some more, as receiving your salary in crypto can be quite the challenge when you first start. The responsibility of converting crypto to fiat currency and managing taxes falls squarely on the employee. It's a process that can be daunting at first, with fears of sending funds to the wrong wallet address and losing your entire salary completely because you clicked the wrong button. Here, the community aspect of crypto companies shines through, as colleagues are often more than willing to guide newcomers through the process. If you have the slightest doubt, don't be afraid to reach out and ask one of your fellow employees to walk you through the conversion process step by step.

Another angle we need to touch upon is the administrative side of things like payroll. Even if it's not all of the time, the pay day can sometimes lag behind. It's not uncommon for there to be delays in salary payments, with employees sometimes receiving their paychecks weeks after the expected date. While these instances are exceptions rather than the norm, they do underscore the importance of flexibility and understanding the startup culture prevalent in the crypto world. You must often adapt to the less structured, more fluid nature of startup operations, which can include irregular pay cycles. This aspect may require a certain level of financial planning and preparedness on your behalf.

Even if payroll isn't as organized as its corporate twin, this industry is known for its lucrative earning opportunities, but also a catch. The high earning potential is often directly tied to the company's performance and the market's conditions of which we'll discuss in the next chapter. As of now, we'll further delve into the crypto company's structure and their compensation packages of which can include performance linked bonuses or token allocations. While these can significantly boost overall earnings, they also introduce a degree of variability and uncertainty, as the value of these bonuses is closely tied to external market factors. It's always best to request higher performance-based commissions than company shares, as you and only you can influence them. If you do happen to receive tokens as part of your compensation, understanding token economics (Tokenomics) becomes crucial. The value of these tokens can be influenced by a myriad of factors, including the project's success, market trends, and investor sentiment. Be sure to do your homework on this, as tokens can literally go from zero to one million, then back down again.

When entering the crypto job market, understanding how to negotiate your compensation package is key. Given the industry's unique dynamics, you'll need to be savvy about evaluating the complete package on offer. It's essential to strike the right balance between a stable base salary and the potential upside of equity or tokens. While the latter can offer significant long-term benefits, they also carry more risk. Understanding the company's trajectory, market positioning, and the potential value of its equity or tokens is crucial in making informed decisions. Prior to accepting an offer, conducting thorough research on the company's background, market reputation, and growth potential is vital. This includes understanding their business model, funding status, product viability, market competition, and exit strategy or long-term goals. If you're lucky enough to receive a job offer, they may require prompt decision-making. This fast-paced environment can pressure candidates to make quick decisions, hence emphasizing the importance of being prepared and informed beforehand. Looking ahead, the landscape of crypto compensation is poised to evolve and become more reliable as the industry matures and stabilizes. This evolution may bring more standardized practices and structures, but the core characteristics of variability and performance linkage are likely to remain, especially those based on one's individual performance. As the industry gains more and more mainstream acceptance and regulatory clarity, we may even see more structured and predictable compensation models emerging. However, the innovative and risk-taking spirit of the crypto world will likely continue to influence how salaries and bonuses are structured. Salaries in the crypto industry present a landscape of high potential and variability, reflective of the sector's innovative and risk-taking nature. A great aspect is that even from entry-level positions to senior roles, the compensation packages in crypto offer a unique blend of stability, risk, and reward. For those willing to embrace the risks, the rewards in the crypto industry can be substantial, offering not just monthly financial gains but also the opportunity to become a millionaire within a few years if you're lucky enough!

In this polarizing work environment, it's not just distinguished by unique financial advantages nor captivating management styles. For it is also discerned by pure dynamism, innovation, and a relentless work ethic that sets it apart from the more traditional corporate sectors. The idiosyncratic working environment here is defined by a particular meld of high intensity, great responsibility, with a real feeling of freedom and purpose for each individual working within.

Nonetheless, we must keep in mind the very elements defining the uniqueness of the crypto realm. Often, unpredictable fluctuations are a driving force that influences every aspect of work in crypto, from strategic planning to every day work, regardless of the role you may occupy. Imagine an industry where new technologies and platforms emerge continuously; you find yourself adapting constantly and swiftly staying abreast of such challenges. Aforesaid, working in this sector requires not only technical acumen but also a mindset that embraces continual learning and flexibility, boarding with entrepreneurship. Due to these aspects, companies need to be able to pivot quickly while still adhering to a broader strategic framework. Effective planning and adaptability in such a volatile environment involves preparing for multiple scenarios while implementing robust risk management strategies. This often means planning for market downturns, regulatory changes, and overnight company changes. Reflecting the very decentralized nature of blockchain technology itself, many crypto companies adopt flat hierarchical structures, enabling this prompt maneuvering of all departments. Decision-making authority is often distributed too, further adding to individual autonomy and the unique company reaction time.

By force of habit, we know the omnipresent culture is composed primarily of Wartime features such as hard work and real accountability. Forbye, it also means a culture that prizes innovation and creative problem-solving. Employees are encouraged to be bold while thinking outside the box and proposing novel solutions, of which often leading to rapid company growth and development. Given its global nature, this helps accelerate and push the company expansion even further. Working in crypto also means collaborating with a diverse array of colleagues from different cultures, backgrounds, and sometimes language barriers. It's important to be patient and pay extra attention when commuting, as seldom is the English language spoken to perfection. This diversity fuels creativity and fosters a more diverse approach to problem-solving, thanks to the people operating within. The prevalence of this remote aspect challenges employees to develop not only effective communication strategies but also flexibility. At times you may have to wear multiple hats, especially in the early stage startups. A typical day might involve juggling various roles and helping out with other tasks on top of your own, necessitating the attitude of a high-level team player while boasting a versatile skill set and a proactive approach. It's capital you keep up with the rapid pace of information and market movements. Instead of waking up early and reading the *Wall Street Journal* to find out the latest price fluctuations of the SP500, here you'll likely be checking the price of BTC and ETH as you sip your morning coffee. Being on top of all new industry trends is a critical part of working in this industry, regardless of your role. Web3 offers many substitutes for the *Wall Street Journal*, namely CoinTelegraph,

Cointribune, or even CoinDesk, each of them offering the latest news on the daily endeavors of our industry. By browsing the above news sources, you'll get all of the latest news, market trends, and internal updates, ensuring that you're well informed and prepared for the day ahead.

Given the fast-paced nature of the industry, your typical workday in this space can be unpredictable. So you really do need to be ready to respond to sudden market changes, company pivots, or client urgencies. Whether it's through virtual meetings, real-time chat, or the more traditional communication channels, constant interaction with other fellow team members is a staple of working in crypto. This connectivity fosters a powerful, dynamic, and hyperresponsive work environment for all the participants. Even if the high stakes and fast pace of crypto can lead to intense work periods, it's worth it. You can develop and learn strategies to cope with stress if you need, and dear colleagues can take a load off if you're overwhelmed to help maintain your productivity without burnout. Embracing other agile methodologies allows for greater work resilience and responsiveness. Focusing on prioritizing tasks and maintaining a focus on impactful outcomes can also be an alleviator of stress, hence enhancing your entire experience in Web3. You'll often be confronted with the challenge of blurred lines between personal and professional life, while setting boundaries is sometimes delicate. Much like in all high paying corporate jobs, there may be some overlapping of work hours with personal life from time to time. Be sure to create a dedicated workspace at home and full schedule transparency with colleagues and superiors so they may help with any unexpected situations.

In the more traditional corporate world, the importance of employee well-being and mental health is central to all companies' policies. In the crypto sector, it's quite the opposite. Don't expect lovely Human Resource personnel to jump to your rescue if you're having a hard day or haven't taken a vacation in six months. The only way you can survive long term in this industry is by transforming your stress into passion and the utmost desire to make a difference.

Spearheaded by this fierce passion and desire to change the immutable, employees in positions of leadership must be able to navigate rapid changes and make swift decisions not just for themselves but for entire teams and divisions. If such a position is bestowed upon you, it's imperative that you adopt a leadership style that is flexible, clear, and most importantly respected by other colleagues. Without the respect of your peers, even the most advanced of management techniques will not suffice to motivate and drive your division. When respected, not feared, your colleagues will actually be willing to work overtime just to help you attain your objective. While demonstrating true leadership is vital in driving teams, leaders also need to be grounded in reality, understanding the practical challenges and limitations of their teams and the market environment to best pivot strategies and layout realistic KPIs. Instigating resilience within teams is crucial. Leaders play a key role in developing a culture where challenges are viewed as opportunities for growth and learning, not for being sanctioned due to missing unrealistic goals. Great leaders in crypto companies encourage innovation by creating an environment where new ideas are welcomed and, if reasonable, explored. This involves providing teams with the resources and freedom to experiment and take calculated risks, which is capital to have an overachieving division.

Over time, you will develop a deep understanding of blockchain technology, cryptocurrency markets, and the regulatory complexities this sector faces. Working in crypto requires a high degree of dedication and tremendous patience. Be sure to leave any ego at the door and approach the opportunity as follows: "One critic is worth a thousand compliments." If you're able to abide by such a philosophy, your crypto job will blossom into a stellar career filled with unimaginable rewards and financial freedom.

CHAPTER 7

Preparing for a Crypto Job Interview

Having the right knowledge, skill set, ethics, and motivation to work in the field of crypto doesn't automatically guarantee you a spot among the select few working full time in this industry. Prior to demonstrating all of the above during your first interview, you need to be selected, prepared, and organized so you may do just that. Like when applying for any job, it can be a heavy, time-consuming task, but even more so in crypto. The crypto industry is still much smaller than all of the other fields, which means that even if the industry is growing, hence the number of job positions too, there's still more individuals looking for jobs rather than positions available. This reinforces the environment of a hyper-competitive job market for his industry. In order to compete in this environment, you need to have the edge over the other candidates and this starts with preparing for your crypto job interview.

Building a Crypto CV

The first step to obtaining a job in crypto is to make your profile attractive, and by the way, this may be said when applying for a job in absolutely any sector. After spending hours job hunting, the next logical step you will have to take is to submit your candidature, hence at a minimum your CV. Much

© Alexander Rees-Evans 2024
A. Rees-Evans, *So You Want to Work in Crypto*,
https://doi.org/10.1007/979-8-8688-0503-5_7

like meeting someone in person for the very first time, that first impression is extremely important. Your CV is but the extension/reflection of your own persona, experiences, and profile; this document will undoubtedly cast that very first impression of your person onto the recruiter, making that very instant they browse your CV a make it or break it moment. Creating a well-structured Curriculum Vitae doesn't necessarily require the use of thaumaturgic skills; it's actually quite the opposite. On the other hand, it really is quite astonishing the amount of bland, complex, and weak CVs prepared by job seekers in this industry. Although you may have the skills and profile for the job position, if your CV doesn't convey that in a simple yet efficient way, the recruiter may simply put it aside and never contact you. On the other hand, you may very well think that you have, as a matter of fact, perfected this and don't need to read the remainder of this segment. If that be the case, be assured that during the next couple of pages, you will find more than one piece of information useful that will dramatically increase your results when crafting your next Curriculum Vitae for your dream crypto job! In the following section, we will hence start by enumerating the main stages to construct your Curriculum Vitae:

1) Format

   The format of your CV is of immense importance and often provides a glimpse into your own personality, organization skills, and efficiency. Recruiters sometimes go through hundreds of CVs sent to them by candidates, all trying to get that same job opening. If your CV is messy or hard to locate certain information, it can result in immediate dismissal as recruiters don't have the time to dissect your document. The format of any CV must always start by considering three main components: chronology, functionality, and clarity.

- Chronology means that all of your work experiences should be listed in reverse chronological order.

- Functionality by design refers to how well a reader can navigate your CV and structure.

- Clarity refers to how easy it is for someone to understand the content, phrases, grammar, and wording of your CV.

It's important to note that recruiters hate overcomplicated CVs in PDF format as often, if they classify you as their client, they like to remove your name among other sensitive information prior to sending it to the employer. If you do wish to make a recruiter's life as easy as possible, do send your CV in both Word and PDF format if you have a chance. To provide you with a very simplistic yet highly appreciated format for such a CV, Figure 7-1 is an example of the way to go.

Name
Address
01234 000000 • 0113 000 0000 • name@mail.com

Personal statement

A conscientious and professional personal assistant with extensive experience in administration, PA and secretarial roles, currently seeking a new position as an Executive PA. A highly organised and efficient individual, whose thorough and precise approach to projects has yielded excellent results. Recent achievements with my current employer include the implementation of an innovative new filing and indexing system.

Key Skills

- 80 words per minute typing
- Proficiency in all areas of Microsoft Office, including Access, Excel, Word and PowerPoint
- Excellent communication skills, both written and verbal
- Accredited member of APA (Association of Personal Assistants)
- Fully qualified first-aider

Employment History

PA to Personnel Manager, Company Name, Location
(April 2011 – Present)

Achievements and responsibilities:

- Implemented a change of stationery supplier, reducing costs by 20%
- Reorganised the meeting booking process, implementing an online system which all staff can access, leading to reduced diary conflicts within the team
- Devised and implemented a new filing and indexing system for files, resulting in greater ease of access and a more time-efficient process
- Helped provide a safer workplace by cataloguing and dispatching health and safety information and posters for the whole company
- Diary management, typing correspondence and documents, creating presentations and creating meeting minutes

Front of House Receptionist, Company Name, Location
(June 2010 – April 2011)

Achievements and responsibilities:

- Presenting a professional and friendly first impression of the firm to all visitors and clients
- Managing incoming phone calls and mail
- Organising stationery orders and liaising with suppliers to meet business requests
- Replenishing and restocking the bar, always ensuring high level of stock management efficiency
- Also assumed the role of fire/health and safety officer for the entire office staff

Secretary, Company Name, Location
(October 2007 – May 2010)

Achievements and responsibilities:

- Maintaining and organising the company filing system
- Answering incoming calls
- Typing all necessary documents and correspondence as required
- Printing any supplementary notes as required
- Running professional errands

Education

College/School Name
(September 2004 – June 2006)

A-levels:
- General Studies – B
- English – C
- Mathematics – C

School Name
(September 1998 – June 2004)

10 GCSEs, grade A-C, including Maths and English

Hobbies & Interests

I am involved in a local amateur dramatics society, where I volunteer as a lighting and sound technician. I have been involved with this society for three years and very much enjoy being part of the team. More recently, I assumed the role of Stage Manager for a two week production and relished the chance to take control of performances and react to a high-pressure environment.

References

References are available upon request.

Figure 7-1. *This CV is simple, straight to the point, and informative*

This type of CV works really well if you're speaking with an independent recruitment agency or headhunters, as they can easily remove any information they don't wish to disclose to the employer. Furthermore, they have a very simplistic yet efficient document in their hands, enabling them to organize information much easier. This type of CV is your best bet when engaging with recruiters directly, as the easier you make their lives, the more prone they'll be to finding a matching employer.

On the other hand, not all CVs are the same, and that's how it should be; however, the structure must always consider the above components. If you're one of those individuals who just likes to stand out and are sending your CV to employers directly, then the following, much more elaborate CV style may be for you. The following example shows the naked structure that a well-crafted, original CV must boast. As shown in Figure 7-2, there's a spot reserved for a photo/headshot, and although it's not mandatory, a nice professional headshot only costs around $30 USD and can propel your image to the next level, instantly creating a C-level-like feel to your persona. This is all part of the perceived value you must be able to convey through the A4 piece of paper we refer to as your CV.

NAME

PROFFESSION

Headshot

PROFILE

Short Bio

CONTACT

- LinkedIn profile :
  Link

- Email Address :
  Link

- Telegram handle :
  Link

- Phone number :
  Link

EDUCATION

School/university name
Name of diploma
Year

Languages
-

SKILLS

1st most important skill for the job

2nd most important skill for the job

3rd most important skill for the job

EXPERIENCE

JOB TITLE AND COMPANY NAME
start to end date
- Responsibilities and achievements

JOB TITLE AND COMPANY NAME
start to end date
- Responsibilities and achievements

JOB TITLE AND COMPANY NAME
start to end date
- Responsibilities and achievements

JOB TITLE AND COMPANY NAME
start to end date
- Responsibilities and achievements

Figure 7-2. *This CV is structurally sound but still missing some things*

Another very noticeable feature on this CV is that there's color. This can be useful to help make your CV more memorable than the others, as the recruiter will probably only have one dark green CV. If you wish to really take this concept to the limit, you can research some color significations, such as how red is often associated with energy and action, blue being loyal and stable, green welcoming and soothing, or even black as authoritative and elegant.

Although the above structural CV paints a good picture, we'll briefly carry on enumerating the remaining components to have a complete one.

2) Contact information

The full spectrum of information covered under this part is composed of your:

- Full name (Be sure to write your first name, then your second/third name. In that order)

- Phone number (Always state either the country or country code alongside the number)

- Email address (Make sure it looks professional and not immature)

- Telegram handle (Telegram is the most used communication tool in the crypto industry)

- LinkedIn profile (If you have a solid profile, it's worth it)

- Address (Optional)

3) Professional bio

Try to keep it no longer than three sentences long. Do use elegant wording, and the goal is to give a high-level summary of what you do in the professional world. If you don't have any experience in crypto, then mention any transferable skills you may have.

4) Work experience

Always enumerate your work experiences in reverse chronological order. Split each experience into a minimum of three parts as follows (By the way, if you have a jumpy CV, try to mention the reason after leaving your prior company after just a couple of months; always make the reasons appear logical):

– Job title and company name

– Dates of employment

– Responsibilities and achievements by short yet concise bullet points

5) Education

Just like the work experience section, dedicate a space on your CV to place your educational background once again in reverse chronological order. Use the same structure by creating three parts per diploma:

– Name of diploma and establishment where it was obtained

– Year of obtention

– Honors, awards, or other prestigious titles obtained during that course

6) Skill set

It's also important to include a list of separate but relevant skills to the job position you're applying for. If you're applying to be a developer, cite the codes you're capable of working with, a sales manager, the types of negotiations you're comfortable with, or a PR lead, the types of marketing you specialize in. Try and keep this content to no more than five skills, and if some are completely different, you can always organize them by family, such as two under a "tech" title and three under "negotiations" as an example. Finally, always mention success cases such as exceeding sales targets, top performer, employee of the year, successfully negotiated a $2,000,000 USD deal, etc.

7) Hobbies

Many people often leave this part out, thinking it's somewhat of an immature category to add, depending on the content, it can actually be a very valuable asset to include. The majority of companies in this industry strive for greatness and believe that someone who's practiced sports (especially at a high level) has a champion's mindset that can uplift the company's performance. If you play an instrument at a small venue, it shows that you have discipline, perseverance, and a winning mindset. Whatever great achievements you have that aren't work-related, include them in this segment.

8) References

Strong references can also be a powerful form
of leverage on your CV. Only add them if they're
impressive individuals/companies, you're on good
terms, and they allow you to reference them.

9) Publications

If you have ever created published content or
participated in published content, do add it. This
will bring even more credibility to your capabilities
while putting forward an argument of authority if
the subject is relevant. Once you've been able to
compile and then place all of the above information
on your structured CV, depending on your choice
of style, colors, and job position you're searching
for, you should end up with something looking like
Figure 7-3.

JAMES SMITH

WEB3 BUSINESS DEVELOPER

PROFILE

Experienced business developer with over 5 years of experience. Competences from Start-ups to Fortune 500s with a passion for Web3.

CONTACT

- **LinkedIn profile :**
  www.linkedin.com/in/james smith
- **Email Address :**
  Jamessmith.gmail.com
- **Telegram handle :**
  @jamessmith

EDUCATION

European university of Geneva
Bachelor of economy
2007

Languages
- English
- Russian
- Spanish
- French

SKILLS

Business development

Networking

Sales

EXPERIENCE

BD AND SALES AT NIKE
May 2022 - Current

- Led the pivot from a product with no PMF to agency business model.
- Created a service offering and generated close to mid-six figures in revenue (started at $0).
- Launched projects other international brands and agencies.
- Created and optimized agency processes (discovery, development, delivery) and cross-functional communication.

STARTUP SUCCESS MANAGER AT TECHSTARS
Nov 2020- Feb 2022

- Oversaw 4 investments: 1 frozen, 2 failures, 1 success (an innovative residential property management company that grew to over 1.5 million sq. meters under management in 2 years).
- Coordinated and contributed to budget, strategy, and team formation to ensure startups viability.
- Did legal work and contract negotiations.

BUSINESS DEVELOPMENT AT SAMSUNG
Oct 2021 – May 2022

- Contributed to growth of sales in the USA (15 million per month to 400 million in 5 months).
- Onboarded 4 major KOLs and 10+ smaller partners in the CIS region.
- Planned and implemented user acquisition campaigns for partners on YouTube and Telegram.
- Helped launch retention and activation email marketing campaigns.

TRADITIONAL FINANCE, SALES & TRADING CAREER
2017-2020

Started my career as an analyst at a hedge fund & trader assistant. Later I joined a car dealership selling emblematic Soviet 4x4 vehicles to wealthy individuals in Mexico and sourced and helped close the biggest B2B deal (sold 19 cars to a resort operator). I I also traded US stocks for 1.5 years with my own capital and learned a lot of lessons.

Figure 7-3. *The CV is now functional, clear, and chronologically correct with a pinch of liveliness thanks to the colours, fonts, and headshot*

Now, another important factor is that it's not because you made one perfect CV that you can simply send it to all of the recruiters heading up recruitment for completely different positions. As you'll most likely be applying for your first job in this industry, you can't be too picky. Although you may want to manage a team of artists in a crypto marketing firm, you may have to start as an artist in that very firm prior to evolving your career to that c-level position. For this reason, it's wise to cast a large net so you're sure to capture something, and in the best-case scenario, you have the luxury of choosing which position you want to accept. To prepare for this strategy, prepare two or three different CVs where each one has been slightly tweaked for specific positions. Have one where you downplay your competencies slightly so as not to scare off more junior positions, one where you make yourself look as senior and experienced as possible to send to the very large openings, and just like Goldilocks, one in the middle that's just right. In all three, be sure that on top of the core content, each one conveys honesty, a champion mentality, tenacity, and start-up experience if possible.

By starting off your job hunt this way, it can mean a little bit of extra work in the beginning but save you immense amounts of time as you go along. Furthermore, it will drastically increase your chances of getting a job in the crypto industry, as for each position you will apply for, your approach will be somewhat tailored to the recruiter's checklist.

Where to Look for Crypto Jobs

As of today, there's about an 80% increase in job positions in the crypto sector, noting that the majority of the world still hasn't embraced this industry. Although the number of available job positions is growing by the day, finding an opening can still remain quite challenging. In the traditional sectors of work, finding and then applying for jobs can be quite easy thanks to the many recruitment websites such as Indeed, Glassdoor, or Monster. Many more similar recruitment sites can be easily found if you simply scroll to the next page of your Google search. Finding job openings in the normal world isn't that hard; however, finding job openings in the crypto realm can be quite the challenge if you don't know where to look. Even if some crypto positions do pop up on the rare occasion on the above-cited recruitment sites, seldom do you have a large pool of choice. These traditional recruitment sites just don't specialize in recruiting for the crypto industry, and it's for this very reason that you must know how and where to search for available openings in Web3.

In this segment, we'll walk through some of the most efficient Web3 recruitment websites, specialized in just that:

1) Company name | Cryptocurrency Jobs

    - Website | `https://cryptocurrencyjobs.co`

    - Specialization | Cryptocurrency, Blockchain, and Web3 jobs

    - Listings | Over 15,000 jobs from over 2,000 companies

    - User experience | Friendly and easy to navigate with detailed job positions

    - Geographics | Jobs from all around the world

    - Application process | Seamless and you can upload your own CV

    - Company reviews | Yes

    - Job alerts | Yes (via e-mail)

    - Salary information | Often

    - Additional features | Community support and career advice

2) Company name | CryptoJobsList

- Website | `https://cryptojobslist.com`

- Specialization | Cryptocurrency, Blockchain, and Web3 jobs

- Listings | One of the largest job pools out of the crypto industry

- User experience | Friendly and easy to navigate with detailed job positions

- Geographics | Jobs from all around the world

- Application process | Seamless and you can upload your own CV

- Company reviews | Yes

- Job alerts | Yes (via e-mail and only from the job categories you select)

- Salary information | Yes

- Additional features | Community support and regular updates on industry news and trends

3) Company name | Crypto Jobs

- Website | `https://crypto.jobs`

- Specialization | Cryptocurrency, Blockchain, and Web3 jobs

- Listings | Very large spectrum but some positions can be outdated

- User experience | Friendly and easy to navigate with detailed job positions

- Geographics | Jobs from all around the world

- Application process | Seamless

- Company reviews | No but company information is often made available

- Job alerts | Yes (via e-mail for new openings)

- Salary information | Often

- Additional features | Community forums and industry updates

4) Company name | Web3 Jobs

    - Website | `https://web3.career`

    - Specialization | Cryptocurrency, Blockchain, and Web3 jobs

    - Listings | More for seasoned crypto employees

    - User experience | Friendly and easy to navigate and advanced search filters

    - Geographics | Jobs from all around the world

    - Application process | Seamless

    - Company reviews | Yes (extremely detailed information on each company)

    - Job alerts | Yes (via e-mail)

    - Salary information | Yes

    - Additional features | Interview preparation tools and educational resources

5) Company name | BeinCrypto Jobs

    - Website | `https://beincrypto.com/jobs`

    - Specialization | Cryptocurrency, Blockchain, and Web3 jobs

    - Listings | Large spectrum

    - User experience | Friendly and easy to navigate with detailed job positions

- Geographics | Jobs from all around the world

- Application process | Seamless and you can upload your own CV

- Company reviews | Yes

- Job alerts | Yes (via e-mail)

- Salary information | Often

- Additional features | Personalized job recommendations and industry news

6) Company name | Bitcoin Jobs

- Website | https://bitcoinjobs.com

- Specialization | Cryptocurrency, Blockchain, and Web3 jobs

- Listings | Large spectrum

- User experience | Friendly and easy to navigate with detailed job positions

- Geographics | Jobs from all around the world

- Application process | Seamless and you can upload your own CV

- Company reviews | No

- Job alerts | Yes (via e-mail)

- Salary information | No

- Additional features | Contract management tools and community feedback

7) Company name | Etherlance

   – Website | https://etherlance.io

   – Specialization | Traditional and Web3 jobs

   – Listings | Very large spectrum with many short
     term/freelance openings

   – User experience | Friendly and easy to navigate with
     detailed job positions

   – Geographics | Jobs from all around the world

   – Application process | Seamless and you can upload
     your own CV

   – Company reviews | No

   – Job alerts | Yes (via e-mail)

   – Salary information | Yes

   – Additional features | You can bid your price for every
     job position.

8) Company name | Crypto Recruit

   – Website | https://cryptorecruit.com

   – Specialization | Cryptocurrency, Blockchain, and Web3 jobs

   – Listings | Large spectrum of primarily full-time positions

   – User experience | Friendly and easy to navigate with
     detailed job positions

   – Geographics | Jobs from all around the world

   – Application process | Seamless and you can upload
     your own CV

   – Company reviews | No

- Job alerts I Yes (via e-mail)

- Salary information I Often

- Additional features I CV building tools and interview tips

9) Company name I Plexus

- Website I https://plexusrs.com

- Specialization I Cryptocurrency, Blockchain, and Web3 jobs

- Listings I Large, detailed spectrum

- User experience I Friendly and easy to navigate with detailed job positions

- Geographics I Jobs from all around the world

- Application process I Contact with one of their consultants and you can upload your own CV

- Company reviews I Yes

- Job alerts I Yes (via e-mail)

- Salary information I Yes

- Additional features I Tailored approach, easy communication, career advice, and industry reports

There are, and always will be, more than just the 9 Web3 recruitment websites available to help you find your dream crypto job. There is however one more very important recruitment entity that helps feed talent to the companies and opportunities to those seeking a job. We're of course talking about crypto headhunters, making this our 10th recruitment entity on the list.

Crypto headhunters are the lone wolves of the Web3 recruitment sector. Often, they're tasked by companies to recruit very specific types of individuals for very specific roles. Sometimes they act alone but can also work in small, tight groups or under a company structure to maximize their efficiency. Compared to what you may have initially thought, some of these headhunters have incredible influence and opportunities thanks to their own brand awareness they were able to create in the industry. These very respectable individuals often get some really unique job opportunities too, as they take a much more hands-on approach when taking on a mission from a company. If you come across them, have a chat, as you never know if a great opportunity is awaiting your response!

Although the majority operate without a website or marketplace, there is one place where you can easily find them, and that place is LinkedIn. Simply by playing around with some key words in the search bar, such as "crypto headhunter," "blockchain headhunter," etc., you'll be astonished by the number of headhunters you will actually be able to connect with. Furthermore, as they're the sharks of the recruitment industry, snatching employees from one company and sending them to another, they are only paid if they can match an employee with an employer. This means that they're always on the hunt for new talent, so generally accept any unsolicited friend requests on LinkedIn. Another great feature about headhunters is that they always try to make the most of an opportunity, as the majority of them may only have 1–3 high profile roles to work on per month. If it turns out that they don't have a matching job position for you on the day you engage with them, they will most likely keep your CV if it's interesting and try to find an employer who may be looking to hire someone with such skills. If worse comes to worst and they don't find a match that way, once again they'll most likely keep it and contact you even months further down the line once they have a potential match.

If you browse the recruitment websites we discussed earlier and do a massive outreach via LinkedIn to connect with as many crypto headhunters as possible, you will most likely be directly or indirectly exposed to 99% of all of the available crypto job openings. If you don't have any success after the first month or two, ask for feedback from the crypto headhunters and rectify accordingly. If you still don't have any success after that, it may be that the market conditions and sentiment just aren't good, so virtually no companies are hiring as they're either preparing or are in a bear market. If this be the case, your best bet is to try and bulk up your CV by becoming an ambassador for a project, joining a very early stage project that's still developing their product/service, or even becoming a moderator for a larger project to provide you with some industry experience and get your foot through the door as you wait for the market conditions to improve and get your dream crypto job!

How to Ace Your Crypto Interview

Now that you've created the perfect CV and applied to a few positions on the Web3 recruitment websites, you will more than likely be contacted by one or more of the recruiters to have a formal interview. This is one of the "Make it or break it" phases. Preparing for this critical moment in your venture is of capital importance. In other words, it's not because you made it to this point that it's a done deal; there's still much work to be done to help ensure that you ace this interview. At first glance, it may appear quite simple, as you've more than likely built yourself up through your educational venture or work experience. You may even be quite familiar with job interviews and have partaken in one or two throughout your career; however, crypto job interviews can be very different indeed and require some strategy and planning beforehand. The actual interview is only part of the recruitment process! Yes, there is the point of initial contact, first interview, second interview (of which can even be done in groups with other candidates) all the way up to live quizzes, questions, personality, and cognitive tests. In this segment, we'll dissect all of these components of an average crypto interview process and detail how to prepare and react during all of them.

Out of all of the above components, it only makes sense to start where it all begins, at the very first point of contact from the recruiter. Due to the decentralized global nature of this industry and depending on what company you applied to join, the recruiter may be on the other side of the world and contact you at any given time. Taking time zones into consideration when applying for jobs in crypto is also something to be mindful of. Furthermore, they may reach out to you via email (it's worth keeping an eye on your spam box), LinkedIn, Telegram (although it is rather rare), and finally phone. Often, they do reach out initially by phone to have a quick introductory call. Like we said, this call can happen at any moment of the day, even if you're out and about in a noisy area. Obviously, you won't know that it's the recruiter calling you when an unknown number shows up on your phone screen, so you must show some discernment and think fast. If you have the slightest hunch that the number calling you could be a recruiter, react as such. For example, if you're in the middle of a busy street or your battery is at 1% or 2%, it's heavily recommended not to answer, as first impressions count. You're more than welcome to go about your day and live your life as you wish, but if the recruiter calls you and he can't hear properly due to background noise or your phone dies after two minutes, it doesn't create a good first impression. If you find yourself with a potential recruiter calling you in a similar situation, don't answer and move as fast as possible into a quieter place and/or ask if you can borrow a charger. In 99% of cases, the staff won't say no, especially if you provide them with the context. Once you're in a calm environment and your phone is operational, call them back. If you have the chance, try not to leave it too long to call them back, as they can be very busy and quite hard to get hold of again if they're busy with other candidates.

During this call, the goal of the recruiter is usually to organize a formal interview after asking a few questions such as "Are you still searching for a job?," "Why did you apply for this job?," etc. Generally speaking, this is a relatively easy, fast-going call, but do make sure that you have no background noise, won't be interrupted, and can be heard clearly at all times. Simple things like this can make you stand out from this very first call as it's highly likely that the other candidates will have some background noise and interference, making you stick out positively from that very first contact.

Also, depending on the type and size of the company, they may have pre-planned dates and times for their formal interview, meaning that you have to adapt to their schedule and not the other way around. Once again, by doing this, you'll already come across as flexible and resilient, traits often sought after by recruiters in this industry.

The second step of your interview process will most definitely be a formal interview. Prior to this day, be sure to send a message or preferably email to the recruiter thanking them for their time and enquiring about the organization of the formal interview. Due to different time zones and communication tools, not being 100% sure on them can lead to you not being appropriately equipped to participate in the interview, or arguably worse, missing it altogether. For these reasons, enquire about:

1) Please can you confirm the time of the interview?

2) Please can you confirm the relevant time zone?

3) What is the communication tool of choice (Zoom, Google Meet, Microsoft Teams, etc.)?

Once the above is confirmed, the interview may take place on a one-to-one basis between yourself, the recruiter, and possibly one or two senior company members, or it may be a grouped candidate interview. The first possibility is relatively well known to you if you've ever had a job interview before; however, the second option is rather unique and can be quite destabilizing if you've never done an interview with ten other candidates in the same Zoom room as you. If this be the case, rest assured, you have nothing to worry about as all of the other candidates are just as confused and vulnerable as you are. However, to ensure that you still remain on top of the competition, it's best to prepare and double-check your equipment, environment, and communication tools prior to entering the interview. As soon as the recruiter replies to your email and confirms the communication tool the interview will take place on, you must immediately download it if you don't already have it, set it up correctly, and test it.

Let's say that the interview will finally take place on Google Meet and you've only been using Microsoft Teams in the past; you will have to download it and set it up. This doesn't just mean download it and then use it the next day; this means adding a nice profile picture and your full name to complete your profile. This only takes a few minutes, but if it's not done, it can look very anonymous and bizarre.

Secondly, prepare your environment. Don't be that one person calling from a dark poorly lit room with clutter in the background. This comes across really bad to recruiters and team members so it's best to avoid it. If you don't have the luxury of calling in from a nice designer room or office that's perfectly fine, hop on Google images, or Canva and download or eleven create your own 3D virtual background that you can add to your Google Meet account as a digital background to be used during your calls. When doing this, try to keep it simple and not go overboard with the style or colors, just keep it clean and neutral. Another important feature of your environment is the lighting. Some communication tools do have integrated light enhancers but without a certain amount of surrounding light, they can't do much. If you see that your surrounding lighting isn't enough, try fetching a small table side lamp or two and position them accordingly. Once you've created the ideal environment, try to keep it untouched and if that's not possible, remember what props you used and where you placed them so they can be easily repositioned.

Finally, you must double-check your equipment; this means audio, battery, computer updates, and Internet. If you decide to use an external audio source, such as headphones, try to keep it simple. Bluetooth devices have a funny habit of playing up when you need them most, so just be weary if you're going to use airpods or other wireless headphones. If you do decide to follow that road, make sure that they're synced to your computer and are fully charged. You can also double check that your audio's connected to the communication tool in the settings section and even test it too. Moving on, if you'll be using a laptop, be sure to either charge it or have the charger plugged in on standby without forgetting to check for any updates needed on your laptop or computer. The last component you need to check is your Internet. This doesn't mean that just because it works at that moment, it will work at the same time tomorrow. We've all been in situations where there's a problem with the box and need to reboot or the Internet provider has had an issue with one of the lines. You can't prevent these unfortunate events from happening, but you can prepare for them by simply having a fully charged mobile phone and pre-activating Internet sharing. This way, if during your interview your home Internet defaults, you can simply switch to your phone's wifi and pick the interview back up within a few seconds instead of minutes.

One more tip to ensure optimum communication results during your interview is to ask a friend or colleague to have a live video call with you on that communication tool from his device while you're on yours. This way, you can get a feel of how it works and play around with the different features, such as the mute button, ensuring successful use on your behalf.

Once you've ticked all of the above boxes, make sure that you're ready for the interview 15 minutes before it starts. Again, if you find your computer needing to update itself all of a sudden, you have the bandwidth to do so, then verify your audio and visuals one last time prior to joining the video call.

During your interview, regardless if it's solo or with a group of candidates, be sure to dress the part. There's no need to wear a suit, although you may gain some extra points, but a classic shirt for the men and a nice simple top for the ladies will do just fine. Once the interview starts, act as if you're listening by tilting your head from time to time, as you will stand out amongst the static crowd as the recruiter speaks. When it's your turn to speak, don't forget to click the unmute button before starting, as it shows that this isn't your first rodeo.

Almost every time a recruiter or company team member will ask you to speak for the first time, it will most likely be to introduce yourself. This is something you can train for prior to the interview. You can write down on a piece of paper some of your greatest and relevant achievements, then structure the corpus around them and practice giving that near two-minute speech by yourself or in front of friends and/or family until you get it right. When you do give this short introduction about yourself, speak clearly, with passion and conviction. To perfect the art of speaking, you may even want to read some books or watch some YouTube videos on that topic. Once you're live on that interview call, however, you will be on your own, but if you've prepared sufficiently and acted upon all of the given information in this chapter, you'll have the best possible foundation to ace your crypto job interview!

When the interview is over and a day has passed, always make sure that you follow up with the recruiter and ask for feedback such as "Have you sent my CV to the employer?" yes? no? plus the reasons, especially if you didn't get the position. Only by collecting as much feedback as possible after each attempt will you be able to tweak yourself to the expectations of the recruiters and employers. You'll be surprised at how much you can learn for your next opportunity!

Summary

By combining an eye catchy yet easy-to-handle CV for the recruiter, knowing all of the best places, entities, and platforms to find fresh crypto jobs, and by making a fantastic impression during your interview, you will surely have the upper hand compared to the other candidates. These three steps must not be overlooked nor taken lightly as each one is an imperative to succeed in your crypto interview. If your CV doesn't have the right narrative or structure, you may never make it past the front door. If you don't know where to look for crypto jobs, you may never access an interview. Finally, if you don't know how to prepare and carry yourself through the interview, another candidate will simply take your place. Just like with anything in life, you don't want to be last, if you follow these three steps carefully and take them seriously enough, you'll by far have a better chance of successfully passing your crypto interview than other candidates who haven't.

CHAPTER 8

The Onboarding Process

No matter your educational or professional background, every single job in Web3 requires very unique knowledge that you can only obtain from working in this industry for some time. Even if you pass the first interview with flying colors, you will still be confronted with some new barriers prior to securing your new, respective role, such as acronyms, industry jargon, Blockchain and crypto knowledge, tokenomics, and more. As we've seen, seldom is there just one simple, straightforward interview, just like any traditional company would have. Here, you may have a series of two, three, or even four interviews that can be in clusters with other candidates. During these interviews, you may even be asked to pass a live initial exam, utterly out of the blue! For those of you who excel in an academic environment, this can be quite a challenge, as no time for studying the particular subject beforehand will be granted. Concerning the more introverts of us, having to introduce yourself in front of ten complete strangers can be quite challenging, but on top of that, you may have to speak out in front of all participants to provide your answers. Regardless of your personality type or learning capacity, there's always some preparation you can do beforehand to help provide you with a big head's start compared to the other candidates!

© Alexander Rees-Evans 2024
A. Rees-Evans, *So You Want to Work in Crypto*,
https://doi.org/10.1007/979-8-8688-0503-5_8

Technical Knowledge

The last thing you want is to be asked a question with some words or acronyms in it you just don't understand, solely because you've never heard of them before. Imagine having a conversation about putting a Public Relations (PR) spin on the technical problems of the new rocket engine with Elon Musk when you're the director of marketing for SpaceX. Even if your core job has nothing to do with rocket engineering, you need to at least construe what the general problem of that rocket engine is to be able to start elaborating a positive PR campaign. The same is for the crypto industry; regardless of your job or rank, if you can't comprehend the general consensus of what your company's doing, it will be exceptionally strenuous for you to be able to operate efficiently. Step by step, we're now going to walk through some of the very common dialects, acronyms, technology, terms, and words every individual interested in working in this industry must profoundly understand. In the following sections, we will target such words, starting with some very obvious, but necessary ones.

Blockchain

A decentralized digital ledger, more commonly known as a Blockchain, is a digital database that is maintained by numerous privately owned, high-powered computers located all across the globe. The data within this system is stored in blocks (hence the name Blockchain), using time stamps and secured with strong cryptographics creating an immutable chain of encrypted data. Because the cryptography and time stamps are all safeguarded and organized by predisposed distributed ledger technology, the Blockchain is naturally decentralized. Think Google Docs for example, the fact that multiple people can modify a single document simultaneously, from other sides of the planet is a form of distributed ledger technology. In the case of Blockchain technology, instead of having to share a link to view the Google document, here, anyone can see a transaction once it's completed on the Blockchain. It's a public repository of complete cross-border transparency leveraging decentralized computer power from all over the world.

An interesting fact here is that Blockchain technology isn't eco-friendly, nothing could be further from the truth. In the case of most large miners or validators, if they simply hooked up their hypercomputers to the grid, they would most likely lose money as the cost of the electricity per reward on the Blockchain ratio would simply be too high. The majority of large Bitcoin mining centers or other large Blockchain validators actually use what we call "stranded power." Stranded power means that it's energy that is completely isolated from the main grid. This means that that energy can't be integrated into the supply system for the towns or villages, and is being completely wasted. In the majority of cases the power comes from abandoned hydroelectric dams or it can even be used to help the ecology such as capturing the emissions of flaring sites in the Middle East and using the heat to generate value on the Blockchain!

This technology has actually been around for quite some time; since the 1990s, computer scientist Stuart Haber and physicist W. Scott Stornetta did indeed use cryptographic techniques structured in blocks to render virtually impossible the modification of digital documents. One could say that this was the work that inspired Satoshi Nakamoto to build the infamous Bitcoin Blockchain as we all know it today. Since then, there has been an explosion of new Blockchains emerging, creating a whole plethora of choice, each presenting their own unique attributes. The two main families of Blockchains are generally split into either two families, the Ethereum Virtual Machine (EVM) (Glossary 20) compatible, or non-EVM compatible chains. To provide you with some examples of both, here are some of the major ones with their respective advantages and disadvantages. Let's start with

EVM compatible Blockchains:

1) Ethereum | Token ticker - ETH | Consensus - Proof of Stake (PoS) (Glossary 17)

   Created by Vitalik Buterin in 2015, apart from Bitcoin, this Blockchain possesses the highest Total Value Locked (TVL - Glossary 13) with a whopping $121.26 Billion US Dollars (Largest Blockchains in Crypto Ranked by TVL | CoinMarketCap)

   Advantages:

   – You can build Decentralized Applications (DApps - Glossary 14) on top of it.

   – Scalability

   – Large community

   Disadvantages:

   – Expensive gas fees (Glossary 15)

   – Long block time (Glossary 16)

2) Tron | Token ticker - TRX | Consensus - PoS

   Justin Sun founded this Blockchain in 2017 after stepping down from his role as former Chief representative of Ripple in China. Today, Tron Blockchain has the second largest TVL in the world, which is of $8.34 Billion dollars:

   Advantages:

   – Scalability

   – Low gas fees

   – Large community

– EVM compatible

– DAO (Glossary 18)

– Fast block time

Disadvantages:

– Regulatory uncertainty

– Competition

– Centralization concerns

3) Binance Smart Chain (BSC) | Token ticker - BNB | Consensus - PoW

Built by the largest CEX in the world, Binance, in 2020 they launched this second Blockchain, which today boasts a TVL of $6.05 Billion US Dollars:

Advantages:

– Scalability

– Low gas fees

– Large community

– EVM compatible

– Fast block time

– Grant programs

Disadvantages:

– Regulatory uncertainty

– Competition

– Centralized

4) Arbitrum | Token ticker - ARB | Consensus - AnyTrust Guarantee (Glossary 21)

Relatively new to the industry, Arbitrum started as a school project at Princeton University and was spearheaded by Harry Kalodner. In 2023, it was officially released and has since obtained a TVL of $3.41 Billion US Dollars:

Advantages:

– Scalability

– Low gas fees

– Large community

– EVM compatible

– Fast block time

Disadvantages:

– Relies on trusting validators

– More vulnerable to manipulation

– Competition

5) Avalanche | Token ticker - AVAX | Consensus - Avalanche consensus (Glossary 23)

Designed to remove the pain points of Bitcoin and Ethereum, such as block times and scalability, the Ava Labs company launched the Avalanche mainnet in 2021. Today, they have a TVL of $1.27 Billion US Dollars:

Advantages:

- Scalability

- Low gas fees

- Large community

- EVM compatible

- Fast block time

Disadvantages:

- Validators must stake 2,000 AVAX tokens

- No penalization if a validator makes a mistake

- Competition

6) Polygon | Token ticker - POL | Consensus - PoS

   Originally branded as the MATIC network in 2017, since their Initial Exchange Offering (IEO - Glossary 22) on Binance in 2022, they have rebranded to Polygon. Tody, they have a TVL of $1.12 Billion US Dollars.

   Advantages:

   - Scalability

   - Low gas fees

   - Large community

   - EVM compatible

   - Fast block time

Disadvantages:

– Competition

– Centralized

As for the non-EVM-compatible Blockchains, here are the three main ones you should know about:

1) Solana | Token ticker - SOL | Consensus - PoS and Proof of History (PoH) (Glossary 19)

In 2017, Anatoly Yakovenko became the mastermind of this Blockchain, boasting today TVL of $6.28 Billion US Dollars:

Advantages:

– Scalability

– Low gas fees

– Large community

– Large NFT audience

– Fast block time

Disadvantages:

– Competition

– Regulatory uncertainty

– Requires the use of a special wallet such as Phantom wallet for custody

2) Sui | Token ticker - SUI | Consensus - Delegated PoS

Spearheaded by Evan Cheng, Mysten Labs developed the Sui Blockchain and made it live in 2023. Today, the Sui Blockchain has a TVL of $829 million US Dollars:

Advantages:

– Parallel transaction execution

– Low gas fees

– Fast block time

– Object centric design

– Possibility to sponsor gas fees

Disadvantages:

– Lack of qualified developers to build on Sui

– High energy consumption

– Small community

– Requires the use of a special wallet, such as the Suiet wallet for custody

3) Cardano | Token ticker - ADA | Consensus - PoS approach called Ouroboros

After helping co-found Ethereum, Charles Hoskinson went on to create the Cardano Blockchain in 2017. Today, Cardano has a TVL of $250 million US Dollars:

Advantages:

- Eco-friendly

- Sustainable

- Low gas fees

- Scalability

Disadvantages:

- Small community

- Lack of qualified developers to build on Cardano

- Centralized

- Requires the use of a special wallet such as Atomic wallet

One of the most beautiful traits of the crypto world is that every single day, someone's trying to create something better than the last person; the same may be said for Blockchains. Just because only a few of them have been mentioned above, it doesn't mean that more don't exist, nor does it articulate that the above Blockchains are the best. As of today, the Blockchains cited are simply the most popular at this moment in time. New exciting Blockchains emerge very often, but only a select few are able to obtain the status of the ones we've just touched upon. Building Blockchains can be a very expensive task requiring hundreds of millions of dollars of investment, as not only do they need to be engineered to perfection, they must also boast very large communities to be successful. One of the main problems of Blockchains is exactly this: having active users. You must remember that each Blockchain community is split into one of the two types: EVM-compatible and non-EVM-compatible users.

Blockchain Mechanics

Now that we've mastered the main Blockchains of the industry, understand how they work, and what makes each and every one of them unique, it's time to explore another important component of the Web3 industry, what it is, and how to read a TX#! For those of you who've never done a transaction on the Blockchain before, you may be wondering what this strange arrangement of digital letters and symbols is exactly. Moreover, every single transaction on the Blockchain has one, regardless of the Blockchain, whether it be EVM or non-EVM compatible. If we think carefully about what each and every transaction a Blockchain would have in common, without a doubt you would think of the transaction ID; that's exactly it. The TX# actually refers to the "Transaction hash," itself being representative of a transaction on the Blockchain. Whether you're going to be a lawyer, business developer (commonly known as BD), or even a marketeer in Web3, the chances are your salary will also be paid out in cryptocurrency; think of the TX# as the tracking ID of a wire transfer you would make from your bank account. The only differences here are that the transaction takes place on the Blockchain and it's publicly visible. More often than not, you will engage with a TX# on a much more regular basis than initially expected.

Every transaction on the Blockchain is composed of multiple segments of information. Depending on the Blockchain your transaction will take place on, there will be specific public Blockchain trackers that you will be able to use for each Blockchain. What better way to start the exploration of them by honoring the main Blockchain tracker for Ethereum, Etherscan, one of the most famous and active Blockchains there is of course (https://etherscan.io/tx/0x1d3d2e22fda9508576d3de48b39e1bf 7e618949c82806986206166661e3794c4):

1) Transaction hash

   – ID of the transaction on the Blockchain.

2) Status

   – The status of the transaction.

3) Block

   – Number of the block in which the transaction has been recorded and how many blocks have been formed since the validation block of this transaction.

4) Timestamp

   – Date and time of which the transaction was fulfilled.

5) Transaction action

   – A basic summary of the transaction.

6) From

   – The wallet address sending the digital assets of the transaction.

7) Interacted with (to)

   – The smart contract of the tokens being sent.

8) BEP-20 tokens transferred

   – The detailed summary of the transaction.

9) Value

   – The value of ETH tokens being sent.

10) Transaction fee

   – Amount of gas fees paid for the total transaction in ETH and fiat.

11) Gas price

 – Cost per unit of gas spent for the transaction in ETH and gwei (Glossry 24)

Figure 8-1 is a real example obtained from the public Blockchain tracker Etherscan. The goal is not only to be able to understand the basics of Blockchain literature but also to provide you with the knowledge of how to navigate arising Blockchain technicalities using the main tools, publicly available to anyone around the world who has an Internet connection.

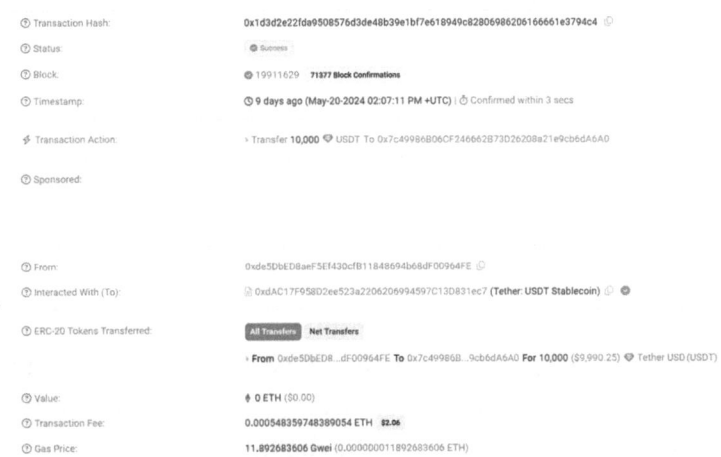

Figure 8-1. *Blockchain transaction information*

We can easily distinguish the different informational segments discussed earlier, each carefully organized and providing very unique insights to help us understand the transaction.

Regardless of the Blockchain or correlating Blockchain tracker you'll be using, almost every single time you will find the majority of the information components we discussed structured in some way or form. A final example of the transaction information placed in a completely different way could be the following example using the Bitcoin Blockchain tracker known as Whale Alert: `https://whale-alert.io/transaction/bitcoin/b0e7dfe24f60c3d5ff1f314899b3f77c60c03a1d0825fb39eef024ad1cc35035.`

1) The Sender's wallet address

   – Wallet address sending the digital assets of the transaction.

2) The Receiver's wallet address

   – Wallet address receiving the digital assets of the transaction.

3) The TX#

   – The ID of the transaction.

4) The gas fee

   – The fee awarded to the miners for validating the transaction.

5) Timestamp

   – The time and date when the transaction was validated.

In appearance, the following transaction example in Figure 8-2 may look much more simple at first glance; however, if we look closely enough, we will see that the TX# is actually correlated with not two but three wallet addresses. The sender's wallet is forwarding the digital assets to two receiving wallet addresses at the same time!

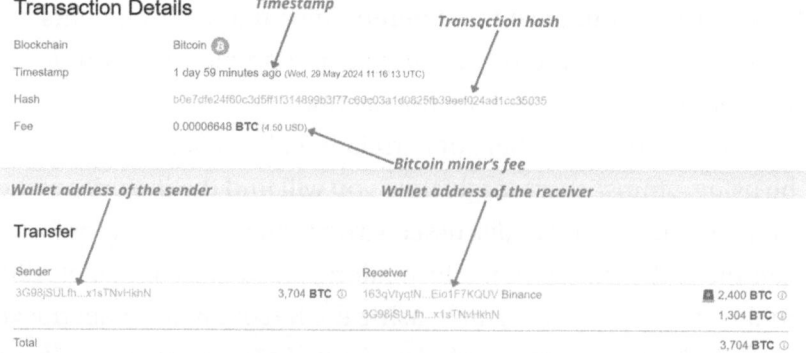

Figure 8-2. *In depth transaction details*

In the above example, we can clearly see the transaction structure and composing parties, having made it possible. In this case, the Sender sent 2400 BTC to one of Binance's wallets, plus 1304 BTC back to their own wallet. The potential reasons for this are indeed numerous, but what such a transaction demonstrates is that smart contacts can be used in very unusual ways and never cease to surprise. Concerning the exact reasons for this bizarre transaction, only the person in control of that sender's wallet will ever know...

Tests

As we've seen, the wonderful world of Blockchain hides a plethora of unknown intricacies, each more exquisite than the other. The many new learning curves encountered through this book are designed to help build up your knowledge and skill set with one ultimate goal: obtain a fantastic job in this revolutionary industry! One of the final obstacles in the way of your exciting new career are the tests. We've learned how to ace your interviews, stand out from the crowd, and build up your Blockchain culture and knowledge; now you'll have to put all of those newly developed competencies to use and pass any tests or exams that may be required. Generally speaking, the larger the Web3 company you work for, the more tests they will ask you to pass, especially exchanges. Depending on your role within your new company, you will most likely have specific tests for your specific job position, so in this chapter, we won't go over each and every one; moreso, we'll go over the two main tests any candidate would have to pass. The Web3 general culture exam and the ethics exam.

Neither of these exams are mandatory; however, if you do have a test you're required to pass, the chances are it will be one of these. Generally speaking, you will have a limited number of tries, usually around two to three. Depending on the scoring system, if you don't get above the minimum required grade after your last try, you will be denied the job.

Even if you passed all of the interview layers with flying colors, you will still be rejected if you fail this last hurdle, which is the last thing you could possibly want. To make sure you ace your tests and do indeed get the luxury of working a high-profile job in this industry, let's elaborate on the details of each one of these tests, starting with the Web3 general culture exam.

Web3 General Culture Exam

This exam can be somewhat of a double-edged sword, as it can make or break your entry into the professional crypto world. Employers like using this test to help the HR departments and principles of the company understand if you have enough general crypto knowledge to work in the industry. Some may say that its sole purpose is to eliminate any candidates whose knowledge of this industry is lacking. Even if you score 100/100, this does not mean that you will be acclaimed, such as Cesar, by the Roman people on your first day of work, nor will it stay in their archives to help them decide when to promote you. It simply means that if you don't meet the minimum grade requirements, you're out. Due to the short time Web3 has been around for, there are not many employees with a great deal of experience. Plus, like in all fields of work, there aren't a lot of employees with experience that are actually very good at what they do. The same may be said here; because of these problems, there's an extreme lack of experienced talent in Web3. Mostly every crypto company has a painstaking fight to find the qualified people, then sift through them until they're able to find the candidates who aren't only qualified but are extremely good. Further adding to this difficulty, not many individuals in the global population today have actual knowledge on everything Blockchain. This is why in our previous chapter, we indulged in some of the more technical aspects of this industry. Now, let us explore some of the general knowledge you will need to make sure you have the best possible chances of succeeding the test!

1) Who created Bitcoin and when?

   – Satoshi Nakamoto in 2009.

2) Who created Ethereum and when?

   – Vitalik Buterin in 2015.

3) What is a wallet?

   – A storage system for your private keys.

4) What is an Altcoin?

   – Every single cryptocurrency apart from Bitcoin.

5) What is a fork (Glossary 25)?

   – A split in the Blockchain's protocol

6) What's a 51% attack?

   – An attack on the Blockchain if a single entity or group controls over 50% of the network.

7) Is it better for a token to have FOMO or FUD?

   – FOMO as it's when people don't want to miss out, FUD would be the worst possible thing to happen to a token; it has the opposite effect of FOMO.

8) Is an NFT a token?

   – Yes, it's a Non-Fungible Token.

9) What's a Soulbound token?

   – It's a token that can't be moved from the entity receiving it. Once received, it can't be moved.

10) What is a DApp?

   – It's a Decentralized application.

11) What do PoS and PoW both have in common?

– They're both consensus mechanisms of Blockchains.

12) What is a node (Glossary 26)?

– A component verifying and authenticating transactions on a Blockchain.

13) What is a hash function?

– A cryptographic algorithm that converts n input into a fixed string of characters and/or digits.

14) What are the types of Initial Coin Offerings (ICO Glossary 27)?

– There are two types of ICOs: IDOs for decentralized exchanges and IEOs for centralized exchanges.

15) What is a Blockchain explorer?

– A tool that allows users to view and search the Blockchain for history, transactions, wallet addresses, among others.

16) What is a Genesis block?

– The first block on a Blockchain.

17) What is a Merkle tree in Blockchain?

– A data structure used to organize large sets of data on a Blockchain.

18) What is zero knowledge proof?

– A method by which one party proves to another party that they know a value without conveying how they know the value.

19) What does DAO stand for?

   – Decentralized Autonomous Organization.

20) What's an orphan block?

   – A block not within the main Blockchain that has been validated almost simultaneously as another, but the other block had more confirmations so becomes the official block, and the validator of the orphan block doesn't get rewarded.

21) What's an uncle block?

   – The same as an orphan block, apart from the fact that the validator still gets rewarded.

22) What does a bridge do?

   – It can bridge digital assets from one blockchain to another.

23) What is an oracle (Glossary 28)?

   – A service connecting smart contracts with an external system enabling Blockchain and real-world interaction.

24) What is a side chain?

   – A separate Blockchain attached to a parent Blockchain, enabling live experimentation and scalability.

25) What does TPS (Glossary 29) stand for?

   – Transactions Per Second.

26) What's the main difference between a DAG (Glossary 30) and a Blockchain?

   – Unlike Blockchains, DAGs don't record data through blocks but through nodes and edges, making DAGs more efficient.

27) What does it mean to burn tokens?

   – To permanently remove tokens from the supply
     to increase scarcity, hence value per remaining token.

28) What is staking (Glossary 31)?

   – Locking up your designated digital assets for a
     predetermined amount of time to earn rewards in return.

29) What is vesting (Glossary 32)?

   – A predetermined and segmented time schedule
     stipulating when and what number of tokens
     individuals are technically allowed to transfer.

30) What's the difference between a sniper bot (Glossary 33)
    and a MV bot/Frontrunner (Glossary 34)?

   – Sniper bots negatively impact tokens when they
     launch; MEV bots/Frontrunners negatively impact
     tokens for their entire lifespan.

With all of this hereby provided information, you should have more than enough general knowledge not just to pass your test but also to accelerate your Web3 immersion. It's always recommended to read articles on what the new trends are from different crypto journals such as Cointribune, Coindesk, Coinbureau, or Cointelegraph. There are other Web3 news outlets that don't start with the word coin, but these four are by far the best. Regardless of which crypto journals or articles you read, be sure to keep the substance varied and the reading regular, as trends can change on a dime in this industry.

Ethics Test

For our next test, the context and reasoning behind it differ immensely from what we've just discussed. The ethics test isn't just another basic filter helping employers gauge your skill set and potential; it's actually got a much more significant role. Due to the lack of any real repercussions for petty crimes in this industry, it sometimes occurs that employees make some very bad choices. One example would be sending their own wallet address to a client instead of the company's wallet address for payment, hence stealing company funds. Another could be to accept bribes in exchange for granting the client better commercial terms and conditions, therefore undermining the company's profits. The list of potential wrongdoings on behalf of a remote employee could go on and on, but you get the point, no Web3 company will start paying very expensive layers to open an international lawsuit to recover $12,000 USD worth of crypto. It's simply not worth the time or effort for such a small amount of digital money. For these reasons, employers are also very cautious of who they hire. One of the main methods they use to vet a candidate's integrity is the ethics exam. You will be asked questions, confronted with scenarios, and confused between your own deontology and honesty. For there is no need to dive into the types of questions and answers in this segment; the answer will always be the same – reply whatever would be in the interest of the company. Not whatever answer is the most ethical or honest. If you can keep the answers aligned with this concept, you should do just fine!

Contracts

Now that you've aced all of your interviews and exams, the next step will be for you to sign your contract! Always ensure that you have a written offer and contract you can sign and agree to. If the company isn't sending you these, it's best to avoid that company altogether. The general process can be one of two ways. Either job offer, employment offer, then sign and return, or employment offer, then sign and return. Also, don't quit your current job until you're sure you've secured a new one. When you secure a new job, you can also send a resignation letter to the current company employing you to transition smoothly. Contracts in Web3 can, however, be very different from the ones provided by the traditional corporate sector. We're all used to having a very sturdy contract with all of the small details naturally embedded within, such as vacation time, health insurance, and others. Seldom will this be the case in Web3. There's always an exception to the rule if you join a relatively large-size firm but you have to remember, the crypto world is one of start-ups, majoritively in wartime mode. They hire individuals to work, not to vacation, so don't be surprised if you don't have any clauses defining your vacation periods. It's also of capital importance that you realize beforehand what you're getting yourself into. Some crypto companies may not even provide you with a detailed contract, let alone vacation time! For these reasons, this segment will shed some light on what to look out for while keeping your expectations germane with reality.

One of the key components for contracts is that they may come in layers, but what exactly do I mean by this? In simple words, you may have a preliminary contract for your trial period, and only once you've triumphed over it will you receive your official, final contract. If this happens to be your case, there's nothing to be suspicious about; it's just one of the many unique industry attributes. Just keep your head down with your eye on the ball, and all will be fine.

Moving on, depending on your role, it's very likely you'll have a non-competition clause or an exclusivity clause. Both mean the same: during your employment with the company, you will not be able to work for or help any other company with similar traits. These clauses can also lead to not being able to have any other job, commonly known as side jobs, even if it's completely irrelevant or different from the one you're about to sign up to. Web3 companies can be very protective about where you spend your time. Even if you have a side job on the weekend or in your own free time, in many cases, the company won't tolerate it and, if found out, can translate into the direct termination of your contract.

Another interesting part of your contract will surely be the jurisdiction where any legal disputes will take place or under the laws of which country the contract is enforced. As it's the world of crypto, very often crypto companies are legally and fiscally domiciled in crypto-friendly countries. As of this moment in time, the most crypto friendly places just so happen to be offshore fiscal paradises or some smaller eastern European countries for the most of them. For these reasons, you will most likely find that your contract resides under the laws of Bermuda, the Cayman Islands, Gibraltar, Lithuania, and sometimes Dubai. If you're thinking of negotiating these parts, it will probably be a waste of time, so more often than not you have to suck in your gut and accept it.

The contract size and depth can vary monumentally too in comparison with other contracts for different roles within the same company. You can find yourself with a three-page contract, highlighting in simple words what the basic terms and conditions are for both parties, or you can find yourself on the receiving end of a ten-pager with exceedingly intricate details. Regardless of the size or depth of the contract, there's one thing you must keep in mind: if something goes wrong, there's virtually nothing you can do. The main components to gauge the quality of your contract are if your role is well specified with all correlating terms and conditions. As long as these are crystal clear, you're off to a good start.

Furthermore, the contract bestowed upon you will more than likely have a confidentiality or Intellectual Property (IP) clause. The Web3 employers take this part very seriously and can often appear highly overprotective on such things. They may even include the protection of their client's IP in this segment too. Due to the very innovative nature of Web3, every individual truly believes that they have a billion dollar idea, even if this couldn't be further from the truth. These hereby clauses are, however, a direct reflection of the true power and value behind the few projects that do indeed have real chances of becoming a billion-dollar company, and once again, even if these clauses seem harsh, there's not really a way around them.

Following suit is your compensation. Depending on what you negotiated prior to receiving your contract, be sure to verify everything you requested compensation-wise is indeed stipulated here. If you have commission on top of your base salary or retainer, do check if the dates and conditions of when your commissions will be paid out are included there too; the last thing you want is to have a misunderstanding here. If you have a token or equity share component too, it's crucial you understand the quantity, US Dollar worth, vesting, and cliff (Glossary 35) periods so you can decide if there is some potential value here for you and, most importantly, when you may unlock that value.

Additionally, there will be a clause stipulating your work hours and possibly the preferred work environment you will need to be in if you work remotely. Depending on the company you work for, they may require that you attend workshops or hackathons on the weekend without compensation. If this is the case, check the small print, and there should be the number of weekends you're obliged to attend these uncompensated events. Usually, it should be no more than the first four weekends. If it is more, it may be worth enquiring about it prior to signing, as in some rare cases, companies can try to exploit their employees by getting them to work for free as often as possible.

Finally, the contract is often signed via Docusign. If you've worked remotely before, this may not come as a change; however, if you haven't, be sure to download the document once it's signed as if you don't and need your email address get's compromised months down the line, you'll have to reach out to the HR department or assistant to ask for the signed copy. On top of this not looking very professional, every department in Web3 is usually very busy, and they may take some time retrieving it. In order to save everyone's time, create a new file on your desktop and just download and add every document the company sends you.

Summary

Be it your technical knowledge, exams, all the way up to the signing of your contract, the onboarding processes may vary tremendously from company to company. There's not one exact science to pre-determine what the specific processes will be until you're informed by the person hiring you. Sometimes you may be put on the spot, other times you may have time to digest and prepare; just remember that whatever part of the onboarding process you're going through, others have done it before. Try to absorb as much information, new terms, trends, and Blockchain knowledge as possible as it will without a doubt give you an edge over all the other candidates.

CHAPTER 9

How to Prepare for Your First Day at Work

In this chapter, we'll delve into the intricacies of what awaits you on your first day in your new crypto job; moreover, we'll look into the necessary steps you must take to ensure success. Many individuals get overconfident and start to relax once they know the job is theirs. In the traditional corporate world, you're not expected to deliver on day one, as you're generally allowed a grace period designed to get you up to speed. In the world of crypto, it's a very different picture… You're expected to perform on day one, and if your performance disappoints, you could be out of a job that fast. Now, let's explore the relative, corroborative particulars.

What's Expected of You

Congratulations! You've landed your first job in crypto. The chances are you'll be enjoying the luxuries of working remotely, and maybe you're thinking about treating yourself to a refreshing, digital nomad (Glossary 36) trip in the exotic jungles of Asia. Imagine yourself renting a luxurious villa with an infinity pool overlooking the tropical wildlife while hopping in and out of calls. Or maybe you'll be juggling with your children at home, jumping around in the background as you're trying to keep up the good impression you initially made. But during the planned calls and work

A. Rees-Evans, *So You Want to Work in Crypto*,
https://doi.org/10.1007/979-8-8688-0503-5_9

loads, you'll be able to spend every second of your time enjoying them while they're young, which is one of the most precious benefits from working remotely. Either way, you've made it! You secured a job in one of the most exciting sectors the current world has to offer. For sure, do enjoy this victory, but don't go overboard with the celebration, as now, the real work will start. You will be pushed into the deep end of a very demanding new job position in a wartime company. This is not the same as starting a new job position in the traditional corporate world, where you will have a nice, gentle start until you're up to speed. There won't be fetching cups of coffee and chatting with the other staff members to get to know them more. Here, you will not be asked but expected to perform on your very first day.

Depending on the job position and company you work for, you may be required to attend a large, team video meeting early in the morning with all of the team leaders, C-levels, and other employees, where some will be required to speak. Generally the team leads debrief on the state of business in their respective departments alongside any complexities or events all should be aware of. During this meeting, there are high chances they will ask you to present yourself in front of everyone. Even if it's a video conference, there can be around 30 individuals attending, or even more. Presenting yourself in front of the majority of the company can be quite stressful, especially if you're an introvert. For this presentation, keep it short by giving a very small overview of the most relevant and high-level accomplishments on your behalf, then state your role and department you'll be working in, to finish on a snappy phrase demonstrating your enthusiasm to be working there. Depending on the quality of this introduction, it can be paramount to keeping your position. For instance, if your Internet connection starts to lag, your audio isn't working, or you're not capable of introducing yourself without fumbling the ball, your contract can be terminated on the spot. As we discussed in earlier chapters, verify, verify, verify all of your equipment is working and ready to go before joining the video conference. If you play your cards right, with a clean-cut introduction, not only will you wow the entire team, but you will also get noticed for all of the right reasons by the C-levels. Depending on the exact context of this large company meeting, be sure to absorb as much information as possible, including what's going on in the company, who's in charge of which department, and what the current complexities within each one are.

After you've attended the first meeting of the day, your next probable step will be to join another video conference with your respective department. This time it's much more of a joyful, less harsh environment as you're with your new teammates. Never underestimate the power of your teammates, as all of you are in the exact same boat with almost every time the exact same goals. During this team call, the individual in charge of that department will spend some time going through the status of business with each and every one of you. If you're in an account management team, the subject will likely be checking in on the clients managed by you. The sales team will focus more on the timelines of closing deals, the tech team on the advancement of specific development, marketing on the results of the current campaigns, the operational teams will target more on the deployment of which departments need to increase efficiency, and so on and so forth. You'll probably be asked to give a more in-depth introduction of yourself too, and the team may spend some time asking for more details to get to know you better. What is certain is that you'll be teamed up with your buddy. There are many different titles given to the person charged with helping you onboard, but the main parameter is that they will help you get set up properly and answer any questions you may have. Just like the flickering glimmer of a candle, gracefully piercing the dark of the night, your buddy will help you navigate the nuances of internal protocols and modus operandi. Although your buddy is tasked with helping you get set up, this doesn't mean that they will do it for you, nor does it mean that you have their full attention. Your buddy still has a job to do.

Often, they will hop on yet another video conference with you as soon as your team sync has finished. This is where they will indeed spend some time with you to help start the technical onboarding required for you to be operational. By sharing their screen, they will walk you through the steps of your onboarding process, showing you which tools to communicate with, how the CRM works, where to find the different documentation, and more. However, one of the constraints of working remotely is that they can't do it for you or hold your hand. During this official onboarding process, you will start to understand just how much responsibility and independence have actually been bestowed upon you. Nobody can stand with you behind your computer and guide you or take the lead. Correctly setting up all of the tools required to perform your duties rests solely on you. This part can even be quite frustrating as there's nobody to physically help. The best you can do is to listen and observe what your buddy's walking you through before they need to jump off the call to carry on with their respective job. If this is the case, you can always ask them if it's ok for you to record while they share their screen so you don't need to bother them too much once they leave you. By doing this, you can always rewatch each step carefully by yourself over and over again until you've managed to set everything up! With all of your company accounts finally complete, one often overlooked parameter yet remains: your signature on your new email address. It may seem obvious, but in the midst of all of your tasks, it's very easy to forget. Nothing looks better than a very detailed email signature with your new Telegram handle, email address, job title, company logo, and links to your company's website. To add to the professionalism, you can also add a nice headshot of yourself to your Calendly, Zoom, Discord, Google Meet, and/or Microsoft Teams account without forgetting to add it to your new company email profile. Try to keep these pictures consistent so all that engage with you will see the same picture regardless of the communication tool you're using. This organized layout will paint a very structured and high-level picture of you.

The very last piece to this puzzle of perfection is your virtual background. Even if you have a nice, natural one due to where you live, the goal isn't to show off or stick out too much. In almost every Web3 company, they should have some pre-created virtual backgrounds in accordance with the company's colors, logos, and style. Be sure to ask your buddy to send you them, and when you apply this background, make sure it's mirrored. By this, I mean that you can end up having your background look like it's back to front, making you look somewhat clumsy when you get on calls as everything will be upside down. Try it out on a private video link you can create by yourself before getting on a corporate call with it. This way you have time to rectify the orientation of the background before you engage with clients or the company hierarchy. On the odd chance that your company doesn't have a predetermined virtual background, make one. Be creative and hop on Canva, extract the company's logo from their website, and place it in the corner a pure, clean, and simplistic 3D image. Don't try to be fancy, as it can have the opposite effect, and if it's too over the top, you may be asked to change it to something more simple. If they don't have their own company virtual backgrounds, creating one with their logo can impress and make you look like you're ready to go all in for the company. Details do count.

Once you've set up your company accounts and visuals, there may still be some work left before you're able to indulge in your official line of work. Believe it or not, you may be required to complete some onboarding tests. Yes, I said it; even if you've successfully completed all of the hiring exams and tests, it's very possible that you're required to pass some more internal ones within the first week. Furthermore, passing this next batch of tests may trigger the activation or termination of your contract if such a condition is stipulated. These tests may vary, and you may find yourself with around ten of them lined up with subjects ranging from the company culture to a quiz based on internal documentation, links, or texts you're required to digest. No matter how frustrating or laborious this may sound, rest assured, there's a hack. First of all, you can ask your buddy to join you on a video conference as you complete each and every one of them if they have time; secondly, you can simply ask your other teammates to do the same or to provide you with hints as they've probably passed the same ones before. Finally, if none of the options are available, take a screenshot of every page with your answers prior to submitting. Again, you should be entitled to a few tries. Once you've submitted the test, you should get an automatic reply with your results. If you're lucky, it will show you which ones you got wrong. If this is the case, you can simply change your answers for those questions by asking your team members or doing some quick research on the Internet. Once you start again, you already have all of the other answers; you just need to jot down while amending the ones you got wrong. If the results come back without any clue as to which ones you got wrong, try and ask your teammates for help; if they can't, you have screenshots of every single question you can now try to find by yourself using the Internet. The last option can be quite laborious, but the main objective is to pass the tests, no matter how much effort is required on your behalf.

Upon completion of these internal tests, you'll be in. Finally, you'll be able to start exercising the job you jumped through all of these hoops for and become an official family member of the Web3 community. All that's left to do is report back to your buddy that your onboarding is complete and ask them to send you all the relative documents you'll need to do your job, such as service lists, success cases of the company, pitch decks, contract templates, or any other relative documents needed. Once received, don't spend all day trying to learn them off by heart; this will come with time. To make the most of time, prioritize joining your buddy or teammates on client calls or in their daily activities to get a real understanding of what's expected of you; this is the best way you can get up to speed as fast as possible. Spending as much time as possible observing someone in the same position as yourself will also help you understand the workflow and how to handle it efficiently. This is how you should be spending the first couple of days in your new position. All of the documentation you can read during your free time before or after work.

At the end of the day, your buddy will inform you on what you should do and when, but if they're very busy fulfilling their duty, they won't necessarily offer you too much assistance. The case may be that they just check in with you every so often when they have availability. If this is the case, it may very well be up to you to take the lead and ask them if you can join some calls or observe them in action. Don't be shy to ask. If you don't ask, you may find yourself left behind, not being able to perform a few days down the line as you don't know what to do nor how to do it. The worst that can happen is they say no, but seldom will this be the case. Your buddy and team will become your most important allies during your time at the company, so you might as well try to bond with them from day one. Do this by showing real interest in your new job position so they feel like you're genuinely trying to learn from them and really want to succeed. The more you show enthusiasm, the more they'll try to help you.

Preparation and Tools

Although you may have set up your company accounts and tools properly, depending on your past experiences, you may struggle to use most of them. For in the world of Web3, not only video conference tools are of common use. In many crypto companies, they use a plethora of communication tools, including some of a more corporate nature and some that you would never see being used in a traditional company, such as the gaming platform Discord. In this segment, we're going to not only touch upon the different communication tools you may engage with but also dive into the characteristics of each and every one of them.

Keeping on track with your first day at work, the most important tool you will use is Telegram. Once your corporate account is activated, you need to start organizing and joining relevant groups. By creating a clear structure from day one, your workload will be much easier to digest. By joining a fair number of relevant Telegram groups also, the most relevant trends, news, and announcements should be within an arm's reach. To find these groups, ask your teammates if there are any you recommend, or simply go on the websites of large, relevant entities and find the link to join their Telegram channel. As you follow through, your Telegram content will start filling up like Figure 9-1.

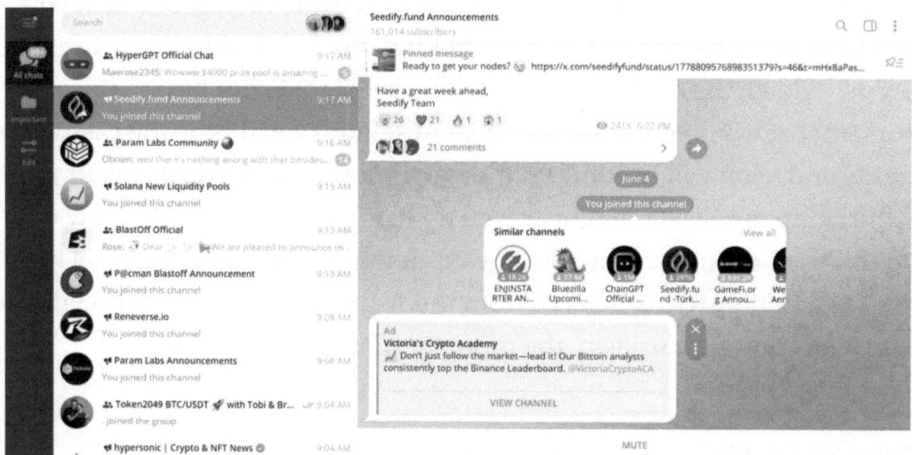

Figure 9-1. *Telegram global layout*

Here, we can see that we've been able to join a variety of different TG announcements, channels, and groups that are relevant to this particular individual.

Now that you're building up content in your TG account, you need to bring some order. This is where the folders come in nice and handy:

As you can see in Figure 9-2, there are different folders with different names ranging from projects to the operations, to the sales department, to the accounts, finishing with the investor folder. Each folder is designed to regroup specific categories of business entities you'll need to either interact with or keep track of.

Regardless of your job position, you will use Telegram in your day-to-day work, so you need to keep it organized. Furthermore, you can create as many folders as you feel necessary and name or classify them as you wish. To start, have at least one folder for each department of the company you may engage with regularly, such as the operations, accounts, investors, and the sales department. Secondly, create a new folder for each new project that you'll be working with, if this is the case. Always create an extra folder containing the main individuals you communicate with on a regular basis, even if you have a private group just between you. No matter what folders you create nor how many, be sure to add all of the relative people, group chats, or channels within each.

The goal of structuring yourself early on this way is to make your life easier whenever you need to engage with anyone or find information. Also, when you attend crypto events or any conferences, you can create a new folder and name it after that specific event with the date. This way, even months down the line, you will always and seamlessly be able to find all of the Telegram handles you collected from that specific event. Not only will this streamline your backlog, but it will also give you a great pool of connections you can reach out to for the next time you attend that event.

Keeping a well-organized Telegram with dates, names, and other clues in the title of each folder will help simplify all of your daily tasks, as you won't always have the luxury of spending precious time trying to find the Telegram handle of a person that you need to contact at that precise moment in time.

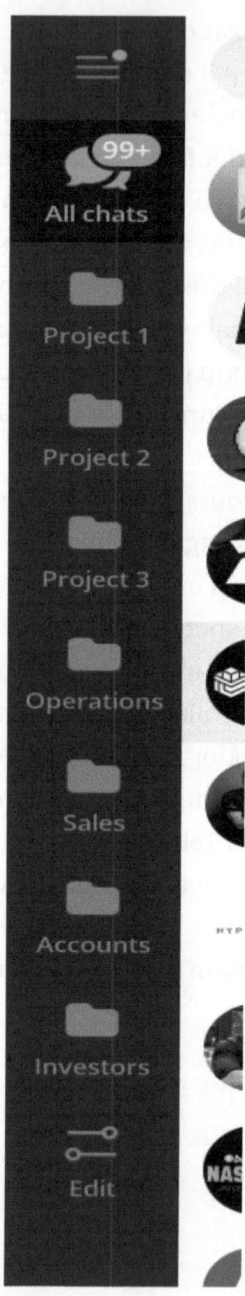

Figure 9-2. *Telegram side bar*

To set a Telegram folder up, nothing could be easier and it only takes a few seconds once you know what you're doing. Start by clicking on the "Edit" label, in this case, at the very bottom of the left panel below all of the folders. Once that's done, the following pop-up window should appear, and all you will have to do is click on the "create new folder" as shown in Figure 9-3.

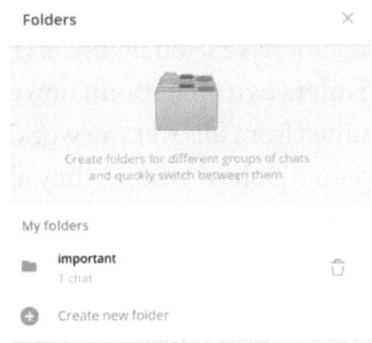

Figure 9-3. *Telegram folder set up*

Now, you will see that pop-up window turn into this one (Figure 9-4). Here, you're free to name your newly created folder however you feel.

New Folder

Folder name

Included chats

➕ Add Chats

Choose chats or types of chats that will appear in this folder.

Figure 9-4. *2nd Telegram window*

You will also notice some other options below, but the only one we're interested in is the "Included chats" segment. By clicking the + sign parallel to "Add chats," you'll be able to add the Telegram handles of any individuals you wish to add to this folder. Once you've added all of the individuals, groups, or channels to this folder, save it by clicking "save" at the bottom right, then "create," once again at the bottom right of your pop up and the folder will be created and ready for use!

Another tool you may not have used before is Discord. This platform was originally used by gamers as a chat room; however, today, it's heavily used by crypto communities from all over the world. Not only do they use it to communicate between different groups, they also use Discord as a place to actively engage with crypto projects. What makes this platform different from all of the other forms of social media is that here, a crypto project promotes engagement activities for their communities where they can earn rewards, whitelist spots for NFT mints, or even get some airdrops depending on the proposed tasks, while the community can hang out in different chat rooms to converse with other members or simply check announcements. Some other differences are that it's far harder for bots to enter and pass themselves off as real users due to the steps required to join the servers, plus you can set up your own servers and rooms where you can have live video conferences between yourselves and other individuals you allow to enter. For this reason, some crypto companies do use Discord to host some of the meetings between departments. If this happens to be the case, you will need to be fully prepared to use this very powerful platform, as a meeting on your first day could very well take place on Discord.

Once you've downloaded the official application from their website, https://discord.com, you will be met by a page to create your account. It's highly recommended that you use your own personal email address to set up your account, as you can get an account banned very easily. Once you've created your account, you will be required to validate it as the platform wants to make sure you're not a bot through systems like Captcha where you have to click you're not a bot then point out which one of the proposed photos is a traffic light, for example. Upon accomplishment of these small verification tasks, you will be immediately taken to your Discord homepage, where you can modify your profile by clicking the clog symbol at the bottom left of your page next to a small pre-set profile picture of your account and start joining all of the appropriate servers you've been asked to join or wish to add simply so you can have a more immersive experience with crypto projects your company works with. This is often when the process becomes a little more complex as it's a very different platform than the usual corporately designed ones. Henceforth, Figure 9-5 will help point out the most important sections, what they do, and where to find them:

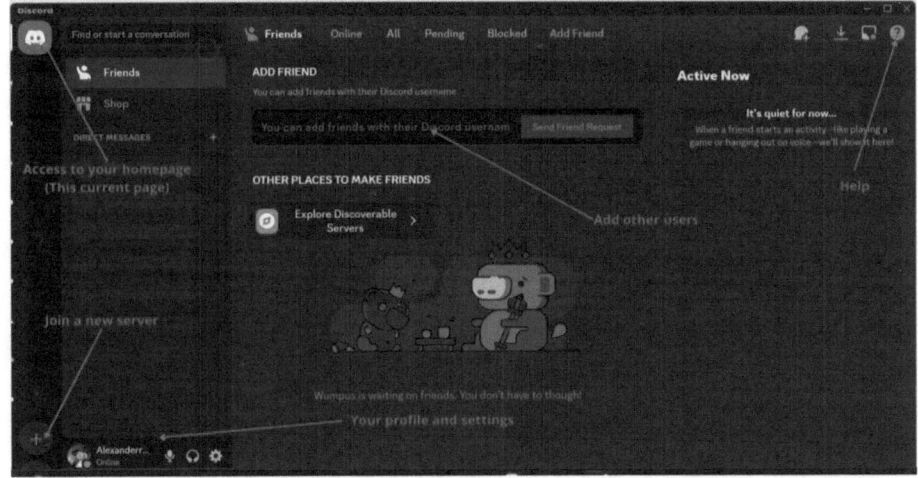

Figure 9-5. *Discord layout*

In this instructive overview of your Discord homepage, we can see the five major sections; considering your account has been set up properly and you don't need any help at this stage, as of now we will focus on the "Join a new server" section. This will enable you to locate then join any specific Discord servers you'll be required to.

This next example shows what your screen will resemble once you've populated your Discord by joining multiple servers and what new sections are made available to us.

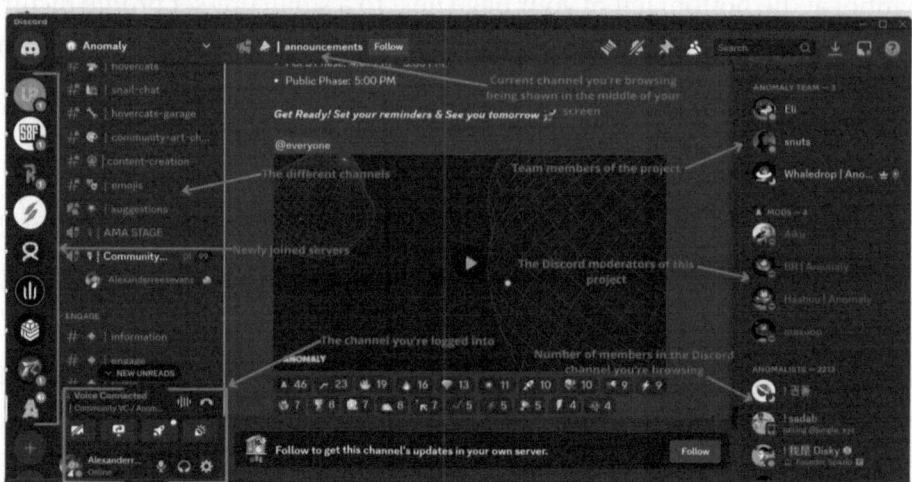

Figure 9-6. *Discord details*

This is what your screen should look like once you've created your account, joined multiple servers, entered one by clicking on it, and logged into a channel where you can participate with video and audio while you've started to simultaneously browse another channel of this server.

Out of the seven segments pointed out in the above image, all but one are self-explanatory. The one that needs some further diving into is the "The channel you're logged into" segment. Put in the spotlight due to the surrounding red brackets, we can see that it's composed of many small icons. Almost every single visible icon in this segment will be vital to a fruitful integration into Discord, that's why Figure 9-7 emphasizes each important icon we can see.

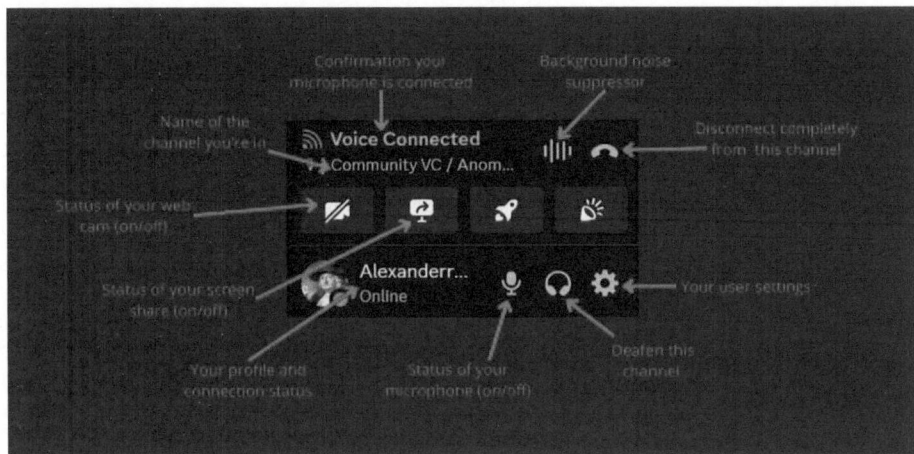

Figure 9-7. *Discord small details*

Make sure that you pay special attention to all of these icons and what they do. One of the more unusual icons here is the "deafen this channel" button. What it actually does is keep you connected to that channel, but turns all communication off so nobody in that channel can hear or see you, nor can you hear or see anything going on in that channel. In some crypto companies that use Discord for some team meetings, they may ask you just to deafen the channel once your meeting is over instead of disconnecting from it completely.

As for all of the other tools you may encounter in your new workplace, such as Slack or Click Up, they're relatively easy to set up and are often organized very differently from company to company. For those of you who've used such tools before, you will have no problem. For those of you who haven't, you may want to watch a quick tutorial on YouTube. Either way, ask your buddy or one of your teammates to walk you around both of them through a video call so they can share their screen.

Finally, what we discussed in Chapter 7 is also very relevant for your first day of work too. Try to gather as much information from the person hiring you as to what tools you'll be using so you may download them and set them up beforehand. Have a play around with the tools you're not so familiar with and don't forget to check your computer for any updates as not doing this may lead to some features not working properly. Get to your calls/video meetings early and check your audio, lighting, and background before you go live.

If you can follow these tips and be on time when every call/video meeting starts, you should be just fine!

Fitting In

So, all of your onboarding is complete, you know how to use all of the required tools and platforms, and are savoring your first day at work, you're off to a great start! All this may be true, but there are multiple departments within the same company and they all have slightly different cultures. Under the umbrella of your team, you're fine and are more than welcome to start bonding with them. However, you may have to engage with some of the other departments which can have a very different vibe and manner of operating than the one you're in. Furthermore, the hierarchy can already be on your back, asking when you'll be operational so you can provide results, and it is possible that one of the assistants hasn't provided you access to all of the virtual spaces you need yet, so you're stuck waiting. Now that you're in the company and fully onboarded, you'll more than likely face some pressure from multiple angles outside of your department and will have to step outside of your comfort zone. This is where you'll have to think quickly and stay under the radar while engaging with multiple departments. This segment isn't really about how you can fit in by making friends; it's more so about how you can fit in your new fast-paced company without being a hindrance.

On your first day at your new crypto job, there are six important traits to exhibit to ensure you become an invaluable asset:

1. Direction

2. Enthusiasm

3. Active research

4. Communication

5. Organization

6. Adaptability

If you follow these sequentially, colleagues won't just accept you, they'll respect you. Let's look at each more closely.

Direction

The most important place to start is knowing what you have to do and when; this is known as direction. Just like when a flock of starlings migrates from Europe to the warmer lands of North Africa, they don't fly blindly at high speeds, spinning, twirling, or dancing above the wrong ocean, hoping they end up in the right place. They rely on their innate migratory guidance system, developed and enhanced generation after generation. Without this marvel of a feature, they would never end up in the plains of North Africa. No matter how fast, high, or far they fly, they would simply exhaust themselves after travelling an immeasurably vast distance in the wrong direction. Imagine if the distance they would have to travel is 2000 miles in a southern direction; now imagine they indeed travel 2000 miles in a western direction instead. Even if they put in the same amount of effort and time, the result is far from positive. The same may be said about your workplace. Even if you put in just as much effort as everyone else, if your direction is off, the result will also be far from positive. By not knowing your direction, you may jump around from department to department and actually start negatively affecting the work your colleagues are trying to get done. This will not only lead to them becoming frustrated but will also create a negative impact on your being in the company, even if you have a very valuable skill set and would actually be great once you're more at ease. Of course you can't know everything on the first day, but that will be your problem, not everyone else's. As harsh as it may sound, that is the truth, and also why you will have a buddy to help. As soon as you've completed your onboarding, ask your buddy for directions. Once you know what you know about your tasks and how to accomplish them, then and only then you can start approaching the different departments, but only if necessary to help complete your given task. To understand your direction, you must also understand your role, responsibilities, and how your performance will be measured.

Enthusiasm

Nobody likes a sulky face or an amorphous soul, especially in the workplace. You have to conceive that the turnover rate of employees in this space is rather high, and seldom do individuals work for the same company for over a couple of years. This means that you'll be in a very dynamic environment where everybody's replaceable. You need to be in your best form and show that you want to be there. From the very first video call, smile and be enthusiastic about being in the company. Whether you're starting at the bottom of the food chain or the top, it doesn't matter; everyone's replaceable, and first impressions count. The second your webcam goes live, smile, look interested, and don't be afraid to tilt your head or use some other body language to show that you're eager to listen to what the speaker has to say. Even if it's boring and doesn't concern you, it doesn't matter; make it look like you're interested. What a lot of people don't think of in this industry is that even if you're all working remotely, you still need to show physical engagement. The majority of the individuals you'll see through their webcams will look completely static; this is not the right way anybody should be presenting themselves while on a video call, but not many even realize that what they're doing has a negative connotation to it. Simply by tilting your head to one side or nodding in agreement from time to time can make a huge difference, as all eyes gazing at the screen will automatically be drawn to you. However, you present yourself, make sure that every time someone sees or hears you, they feel as if you're happy to be there.

Active Research

There will be times when you're on video conferences and you hear terms or see depictions you're not familiar with. Often, there can be an entire conversation emerging from one of these unfamiliar words, and these stressful times will happen more than once during your first few days. As some of the meetings you'll attend can go on for a while, there can be an entire plethora of unknown phrases that will pop up, and if you stack them up until the end to ask your buddy, the chances are that you won't understand anything from the time spent in the meeting. When you work remotely, an undervalued luxury is always at hand, your computer. Never, would you be allowed to whip out your mobile phone to do some research during an important meeting in the boardroom in the corporate world. In Web3, however, you can simply open a new tab on your computer and start your research as the C-level's speaking. They don't need to know this, and if it will help you understand the conversation, do it. Don't use your mobile phone, however, as they will see on the screen that you're looking down instead of at the screen and will without a doubt think that you're playing with your phone instead of listening to them. By doing this active research, it will save you and your buddy a lot of time while making sure you absorb as much information as possible, enabling you to keep up with the pace of the company.

Communication

By making the most of your buddy while you're on a call with them can help a lot. It's during these times that you should ask as many questions as possible, and remember, there's no such thing as a silly question. It's your first day on the job, so it's completely understandable that you don't know everything yet, but do try to find out by yourself at first to avoid wasting time. If you're not able to find out the answers by yourself, the worst thing you can do is withhold any questions you may have, as if you do, a few days down the line you will not be progressing in the right direction. Furthermore, make sure that your questions are concise and don't beat around the bush. This is a big part of working in Web3; you need to be honest and open about everything. Make sure that any and all questions you ask are clearly formulated to be "crystal clear." This means that what you're saying is so clear and concise that even your grandma would understand. The same may be said about written communication too.

Organization

With your potentially overwhelming first day at work, you may very well find yourself losing track of important information. Although taking notes is a basic step in the normal corporate world, here, the pace is so fast that you can forget or simply just not have the time. Regardless of your role, keep a large A4 size notepad at hand. Try not to go too much into details for every piece of information you'll be jotting down, as you will end up getting half way through a sentence and then have to stop and start scribing away at your next note. Try to keep your notes very short but with key words, times, and dates to remind you of the full context. On top of notes, you're very likely to have a full schedule, so make sure you have no imperatives that day, nor for the first couple of weeks if possible. In this industry, it's not at all a norm to take a 2-hour lunch break or pop off to your dental appointment. Even once you've been in the company for a while, these things aren't really accepted unless it really is a one-off. So on your first day at work, you can't leave early to go to your football training, leave in the middle of the day to pick up your kids, or indeed pop off for a medical appointment. Make sure that any imperatives you have are either rescheduled or delegated accordingly. When it comes to organizing your actual work day, your buddy should inform you of what will happen and when. If that's not the case, do ask your buddy or other team members.

Adaptability

As the majority of Web3 companies are in wartime mode, tasks, goals, activities, or even job positions can change at the slide of a hand! This is actually quite an exciting parameter to be considered on your first day of work. You may find out that after introducing yourself in the morning meeting, one of the C-levels decides you'll be a better fit in a different department working in a different role. As odd as this may seem, this isn't uncommon. You need to embrace adaptability and the prospect that events will change without giving you any heads up whatsoever. The question isn't if; it's when such an event occurs, what do you do? The best answer is to go with the flow; don't fight it. Eventually, you will become accustomed to change, as it is an intricate part of working in Web3. Concerning the adaptability aspect of the industry, it's not just the work that can be impacted. In some companies, there can be use of foul language by some of the team or C-levels. Sometimes it can be quite funny depending on the context, other times it can be downright degrading. If you are targeted by such language, there's absolutely no point in trying to file a complaint to the HR department, as they are not there to deal with such problems. Regardless of your sex, you've got to toughen up and wait for it to pass. Never take the verbal abuse personally, as everyone gets their fair share at some point. Take it to the chin and move on.

Fitting in with your new teammates should be easy as long as you don't have any ego. Fitting in with the other departments should be fine as long as you don't bother them too much. Fitting in with the C suite can be done at a slightly later stage, but only if you keep your distance and do your job exceptionally well. On your first day, don't try to make friends with every single person in the company; it won't happen. Stick to your team and make sure you really work hard. The turnover rate of employees in this industry is so high that even if you're generally a really nice person and are getting on well with your team, the ultimate way to fit in is to grind through all of the nitty-gritty thrown at you and still do a good job. By doing this, your teammates alongside other company staff won't just appreciate you, they'll respect you.

Summary

Organization and getting up to speed as fast as possible are capital to having a very successful first day on the job. There will also be times when you need assistance from colleagues or your buddy, don't shy away from help, and don't hesitate to reach out. Immerse yourself in the work of relevant colleagues and try to understand what they're doing, how they're doing it, and more importantly why. Knowing why you're performing a task in a particular manner will enable you to grow rapidly instead of dwelling on ideas that have been tried by others before you. On this first day, try your best to stay low-key, efficient and absorb as much important information as possible. Finally, make sure you correctly check in and check out if your company requires you to do so, and when the end of the work day arrives, it doesn't mean that you have to stop working. If you still have lingering tasks for that day, work over the mandatory company hours to complete them, hence the next morning, you start in applaudable conditions.

CHAPTER 10

How to Keep Your Job

Now that you're fully onboarded in your new crypto job, it doesn't necessarily mean that it's all smooth sailing from here on out. In this space, there's an incredible turnover rate of employees. This isn't to say that they're good or bad; the majority of them, unlike yourself after reading this book, are simply not prepared enough to take on a job in crypto. It's really not unusual to see newly hired employees being made redundant after just a few weeks, or in some extreme cases, a few days, after starting their new position. Majoritarily, these very early redundancies come down to an accumulation of small but irritating mistakes such as Internet problems, not learning fast enough, or never being on time. However, for the later stage ones, it almost always comes down to underperformance. Again, this isn't to say that they aren't competent or qualified enough; they're just not good enough. In this chapter, we'll touch upon every relative aspect to ensure that you are fully prepared to become a long-term player in this field.

Key Performance Indicators (KPIs)

Much like in ordinary corporate jobs, you're hired for a reason – to perform specific tasks meeting the direct needs of the company. Just like the carefully crafted clogs of a Swiss watch, they must all be perfectly synchronized in order for the watch to work correctly. The same may be said for a company. If each employee is carefully handpicked for

© Alexander Rees-Evans 2024
A. Rees-Evans, *So You Want to Work in Crypto*,
https://doi.org/10.1007/979-8-8688-0503-5_10

their specific qualities and all departments are synchronized, then the company will work correctly. If one clog in a watch isn't synchronized or isn't the perfect size or fit, the watch will simply cease to work correctly. Once again, the same principle may be applied to the performance of a company, especially in Web3. Due to the wartime mode they're all in, each employee in each department is there for a reason. Moreover, the majority of companies in Web3 are either small, with anywhere from a handful of employees, or of what's considered a good-sized company in this industry, anything over 50–100 employees. These two company sizes make up the bulk of companies in Web3, and for the larger ones with over 100 employees, they still rely on each and every employee. There's a simple science behind all of this: the larger the company gets, the more departments they'll have. Each department will end up becoming relatively independent, somewhat taking on the responsibilities of a small company. For these reasons, every single employee is of the utmost importance, as each job opening is to fill a real need of the company. Due to the importance of filling each company position with the right person, once you're hired and onboarded, you will not have a lifelong contract. Most likely, you will have objectives to hit every month or so in order to keep your position. This is where you will have to stay on top of a multitude of parameters, of which the first we'll discuss are your KPIs.

A KPI is a metric used by the majority of crypto companies to help gauge your performance, as it says in the name "Key Performance Indicator." Not only is this a simplified performance metric to help the company understand if you're doing your job, it generally entails a specific task you must hit within a predefined period of time. This given time frame is generally stipulated within your contract and varies depending on positions, so it's always good to double check so you understand what yours is. If that's not the case, your KPI may be given to you on your first day of work, so you'll have to pay extra attention to details and complete your onboarding as fast as possible. Either way, you will have a specific target to hit on a monthly basis, and this can determine whether or not you'll keep your job position. As an easy example, let's imagine you'll be a business developer for a crypto marketing firm. Your KPI may be to generate a minimum of 20 hot leads every week. If you're a lawyer for a CEX, your KPI may be to review, amend, and accept 30 new client contracts every two weeks. Or let's imagine that you're a sales manager; you may have a KPI of closing a minimum of $55,000 USD worth of deals every month.

The kaleidoscope of jobs in this industry means that there's different KPIs according to your given role. Each company will create their own KPIs according to their needs. A large CEX such as Binance probably won't list a token on their exchange for under $500,000 USD, so of course, if you're applying to be a sales manager there for your first job, it's most likely they won't hire you unless you have tremendous experience, as their KPIs will probably be very high. This is something you need to anticipate when applying for a job. The more established the company is, the more serious the KPIs will be. It goes without saying that you can't glance into the future and anticipate the KPIs you will have, but you can adapt your candidature applications by aligning them with smaller companies to start building up some experience before trying to enter the big league. Even if you have a stellar CV, make it through all of the hiring rounds, ace your exams, and successfully complete your onboarding, you'll still have KPIs. If you can't keep up with them, it will likely end in the termination of your contract. You may be able to talk the talk, but it's mandatory that you walk the walk. All of that hard work you put in will end up being all for nothing.

Another interesting component about KPIs is that they can evolve over time or the market sentiment; this can be good or bad. If the market is in a Bull run, you may very well find your KPIs increase as there's more to be done. You could be a community manager and all of a sudden find that the community you're managing doubles in just a few weeks. If your KPI is replying to 95% of all of the community members' questions every hour, the bull run can be a problem for you. As your community has doubled in members, you still have to reply to at least 95% of all questions every hour from the aforementioned members. The company may very well start hiring new community managers to take some weight off your shoulders, but that may take time. What nobody in this industry has time for are excuses; whether you're right or wrong, you've been working overtime; none of it matters. The only thing that matters is providing results.

However, if you're on the sales team, a good Bull run should make your life far easier as the whole market is liquid. Even if your KPI is moved from closing $55,000 USD worth of business per month up to $85,000 USD per month, you will have a lot more funded clients ready to buy your product or service as fast as possible so they don't miss out on the Bull run. You will find hitting your KPIs will be a walk in the park, even if they're increased.

On the other hand, in the Bear market, these two scenarios can be inverted. Here, even if the KPIs will be reduced for a sales manager, it will be a constant struggle to find and close business. Imagine your KPI is reduced to $25,000 USD during this period; the market will be dry, and very few potential clients will have funds to purchase your product or service. During this period, you're still not allowed to make excuses, even if what you're saying is true. The company you work for still needs to generate revenue, and you are contracted for doing just that.

Contrary to the sales manager, the community manager will have it far better in the Bearish season, as the number of active community members will slowly but surely diminish as the market sentiment drops. If their community drops from 60,000 individuals to 30,000 individuals, their KPI may even increase to 100% of questions from the community must be answered every hour, but it's still far more feasible than 95% of a 60,000 large community.

Depending on your role, the market conditions and sentiment will affect your capacity to hit your KPIs in very different ways. One great way to stay ahead of the curve, or at least prepare yourself for the challenges your forever evolving KPIs withhold, is to check on a daily basis the market sentiment. The market sentiment paints a very good picture of how people are feeling about the current market. By depicting the appetite of retail investors through their purchasing behavior, social media engagement of projects, and other parameters in the market, we're able to see what the general state of the market is. By observing what we refer to as the Fear and Greed Index (FGI) (Glossary 37), we can understand what the actual market sentiment is, plus look for patterns to help us distinguish trends. The FGI is of outstanding importance as it provides you with what's really going on in the market. As said by the late Peter Drucker, "The best way to predict the future is to create it," and the FGI is as close to creating the future as it gets. Figure 10-1 from Coinstats demonstrates just how accurate the FGI can be (`https://coinstats.app/fear-and-greed/`).

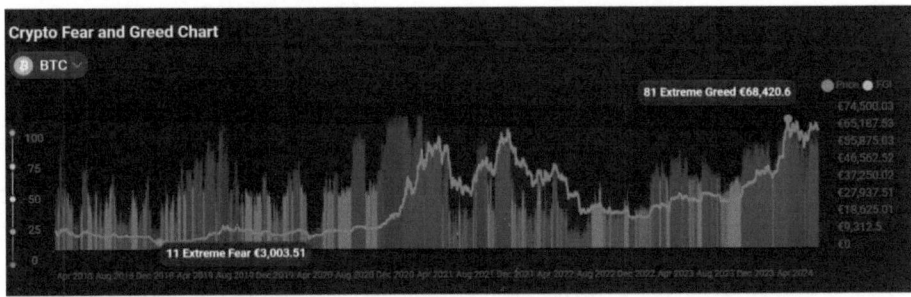

Figure 10-1. *FGI chart*

If we look carefully at the dates on the x-axis, we can clearly see how the Bull run of 2021 correlates perfectly with the hypothesis of the FGI. Furthermore, we can look at the duration that Bull run took place over which started to pick up steam in the beginning of 2021, then started to die down at the end of 2021. Observing the chart with today's metrics, it clearly looks like we're about to hit a Bull run, and judging by the past one, it shouldn't last more than one year. Armed with this knowledge, I can assume my KPIs will likely start to increase in the near future, so I can prepare accordingly by maybe asking the C-levels to hire some more individuals, organize my workload differently, build out strategic partnerships, or simply start clearing my Customer Relationship Management (CRM) tool to enable more bandwidth for new deals.

Assuming you have the skill set to hit your KPIs on a regular basis, make sure to keep up-to-date on the latest trends and market sentiment. By doing this, you will always be one step ahead of the other employees and prepared to hit all of your KPIs, no matter how they evolve!

Critical Hit

As you embark on your curious voyage in the working world of crypto, not only will you have KPIs, you will more than likely have what is known as your critical hit. Unlike your KPIs that you must hit on a regular basis all year round, your critical hit is a one-off. Much like what the name leaves to think, it is a target that you must hit to survive. Some argue that the concept was inspired by the hunting strategies of predators in nature; others argue it originated from a special type of strike in combat/shooter video games. One fatal blow that will eliminate an opponent in a single hit. In the crypto world, there are two types of critical hits you must be aware of: one is given to you by the company, and the other, you and you only can know. In order to keep your job in this action-packed industry, you must be able to master both types of critical hits, but before we go into the details of each, it will be useful to expand on the philosophy behind the infamous critical hit as a whole.

There is without a doubt a deeper meaning going on behind the scenes. Much like a predator in nature such as the apex cheetah, before engaging in hunting down a prey, they calculate the risk that specific hunt entails. Once the prey is identified from a distance, the cheetah will assess the prey in detail, such as the size, age, energy levels, behavior, strength, defense mechanisms such as tusks or horns, and potentially the general awareness of that given animal. Preceding any attempt at a heedless attack, the cheetah will continue to observe the environment of the prey, as there may be rocky terrain, elders of that herd watching over the slipshod offspring as they avidly graze, or maybe even other predators hiding out behind the same prey waiting for just the right moment to pounce. They will also carefully analyze the sunlight, distance, then the force and direction of the wind to not give away their position too soon, until finally they take one final component into consideration, their own status. By becoming aware of their own capacities, energy levels, and injuries, among other parameters, the cheetah will take all of the absorbed information into account, calculate based on its own risk tolerance, and state if the prey is worth pursuing. The cheetah can only be wrong so many times on this internal calculation before it drains itself of all energy reserves and can no longer pursue any prey. When this happens, the predator will simply die of starvation, and the world will go on, all because the animal didn't obtain their "critical hit."

This concept is very much relatable to more or less any job position in the crypto industry. You and only you must know which clients, tasks, or missions are actually attainable. For instance, if you're working as an investment analyst for a VC firm, there's only so many projects you can invest in; moreover, there's only so many you can speak to and assess. Depending on the market cycle and sentiment, there can be thousands of crypto projects launching every month. Seldom will you have the bandwidth to assess each and every one of them before they launch; this is the environment. Also, depending on the vesting schedules and rounds you invest in, even if you track down a great project, it just may not be a fit as you simply don't have the capacity to absorb the wait to liquidate their tokens; this is your status assessment. Finally, the project may be far too small, far too big, or simply only looking for certain pre-desired tier 1 VC firms to invest; this is the assessment of the prey. If you don't take these pre-engagement factors into consideration, you will waste a tremendous amount of time, energy, and effort going after a target with a very high and real risk that nothing will come of it. The result in the wild is that you will drain your life source and perish; here it means that you won't invest any of the funds allocated to your company for investment purposes and will likely have your employment contract terminated. By understanding your target's capacities, the environment, and your own capacities before you start investing your time and energy into pursuing such a given target, you will save tremendous amounts of valuable time that you can place into concluding business with a more fitting target. You need to calculate your risk/return on investment (ROI) ratio. Without going into any complex or long mathematical equations, there's a pretty straightforward formula you can apply whenever you're facing the situation of "to pursue or not to pursue a target."

To start, understand that in our case, risk is the chance that the deal will conclude. This is noted in a percentage format ranging from 0% chance (it will not happen) up to 100% (it's guaranteed to happen). To calculate this percentage, it's better to estimate it, as you understand all of the variables more than any computer ever could.

As an example, let's say that the target client came from a warm introduction, has raised $400,000 USD, has no major investors backing them, and needs to raise another $600,000 USD before listing their token on a CEX 4 weeks from now. The chance that this project will accept an investment from you is probably around 90%, as they're pressed by time, aren't trying to create a tier 1 cap table (Glossary 38) with only reputable VCs, and still have a lot of money left over to raise.

Secondly, the ROI is also shown in a percentage format. The basic calculation for the ROI is: (Profit/investment)x100=ROI

In our case, let's imagine that we invest $200,000 USD with an expected profit of $350,000 USD:

$$(350,000/200,000)x100=175\%$$

Looking at the above numbers, it appears like a very appetizing deal.

With this given example, you have a 90% chance of making a 175% ROI (without taking into consideration the internal risk adjustment calculations). Knowing this, it's obvious that that target is worth pursuing.

In this second case, let's imagine the project has raised $7,750,000 USD out of $8,000,000 USD, they only have tier 1 investors on their cap table and are listing their token in 3 months. Imagine you're working for a tier 2 investment firm; the chances they will accept a ticket from you are probably 10% as they only have a small amount left to raise, only have tier 1 VCs on their cap table, and have plenty of time on their side.

As it's a large, reputable project, their investment terms are less friendly, and your ROI is as follows:

$$(350000/250000)x100=140\%$$

In this latest case, you have a 10% chance of obtaining a 140% ROI on virtually the same initial investment capital.

It goes without saying that from a pure financial perspective, you will be far better off pursuing the first, smaller deal, as you'll have a much higher chance of securing an even higher ROI.

Concerning all of the other job positions where you won't have a tangible number to use as your initial investment to calculate your ROI, you can't replace that part with time or energy you'll be spending. You can however replace it by estimating a number on a scale from 1 to 100, how much time and energy you will have to put in to close the deal, then add or remove the number of zeros so you end up with the same amount of digits as your profit, like follows:

Let's say your client may pay $28,000 USD, but on a scale from 1 to 100 in terms of your time and energy invested, you will be at a 35 as they will need you on two more calls to explain the details to all of their team and board members, don't speak English well, and are in an opposite time zone, but, you can close the deal within the next few days, although it will be intense.

Also, they have the funds to pay for it, your pricing is on par with the competition's, the size of the deal is extremely reasonable, they need your product, and you've built a great relationship with them, so your chance of sealing the deal is 95%. Taking all of this information into account, the ROI would be:

$$(28000/45000)x100=80\%$$

It's important to note that you can't score over 100% for calculating this form of ROI, contrary to a real initial investment, so here we have an extremely high ROI and a 95% chance you'll be able to obtain it. It's important to note that the higher the score you will note down for your time and energy, the lower your ROI will be. It goes without saying that this way of finding an approximate ROI for your time and energy won't be applicable if you have a very unique deal that completely supersedes the norm of your deals. If you have the opportunity to close a deal with a price 10 times greater than the average pricing you seal with, this probably won't reflect the reality of that particular ROI. This calculation is specifically designed to provide you with an idea of ROI for your average day-to-day deals.

As you apply this method, you should start to notice a change in the way you spend time with all prospects and clients. Instead of going after a larger, more complex deal that may take a lot more time, you'll start to focus on much more reasonable targets, hence enhancing your efficiency and profitability immensely.

This is the critical hit of which you, and only you are the undeniable master of and must always carry at the forefront of your working process.

The second critical hit is the one bestowed upon you by the company. For this critical hit is a one-off, immediate task you must complete to secure your position in the company. On top of your ongoing KPIs, which are designed to keep you performing to a certain standard on a regular basis, you will have a completely one-off independent task, of which you may only have seven days to complete. The goal here is not to show the company that you can hit some decent metrics on a regular basis in a reasonably comfortable setting; it is to show the company that you're capable of focusing and hitting that one, time-biased task.

Using the same prior example of the investment analyst, of whom indeed may have a KPI of reviewing $500,000 USD worth of investments every month, it's possible that they have a critical hit of providing analytics reports for 20 projects within the first ten days of them starting their job.

Following the comparison with a predator in nature, we're not asking the cheetah to show us how they survive long term; we're asking them to demonstrate what they're capable of. We're asking them to unleash their full power upon a given target of our choice that they have to take down.

Between these two distinct forms of critical hits, we know that depending on the company you'll work for, you will have a very concise target that you must hit, whatever the costs. You mustn't think about the energy reserves or time you're about to exploit. This critical hit is mandatory for your immediate survival, and you won't be afforded the luxury of choosing your target or a large amount of time for you to carefully plan your strategy and approach. You must put all of your effort into this one task, regardless of the cost, even if you have to burn a small bridge or two.

In contrast, our initial critical hit emits a much deeper, almost philosophical aura. Your own critical hit won't be just a one-off; it will become your strategic ally, guiding you through difficult choices, market conditions, and sentiments. For every task you will undertake, there will always be a myriad of manners in which the bespoke task may be completed. Abiding by the same strategy used by some of nature's deadliest predators will without doubt provide you with a very efficiency-based plan that will help structure your entire career. Is that client really worth going after? Or could you close multiple clients in that same period of time that would result in a higher turnover? All of these questions will be far easier to answer when you use the critical hit approach.

Transparency

Throughout the early pages of this book, we briefly touched upon this subject. We did not, however, dive into the details and the types of transparency you must exhibit throughout your career in Web3. All companies in this industry place transparency high on their list when it comes to employees, and you mustn't forget that your salary will be paid in a form of crypto currency, meaning on the blockchain. What's one of the unique features shared by around 99% of the blockchains out there? They're publicly accessible, so any bribes or behind-the-scenes transactions will eventually be found out. Unlike fiat currencies and bank accounts, your employers can actually check the cryptocurrencies in your wallet, which wallet addresses sent them, and where you sent them too. Furthermore, due to the ubiquitous telecommuting working environment, many individuals working in this industry try to work multiple jobs simultaneously, among other questionable activities. To top all of this, because you'll be more than likely to work remotely, they'll need to be reassured that you're actually working. KPIs do help them verify this, but they'll probably monitor your CRM activity too, as if you're able to just surpass your KPIs on a monthly basis by doing the bare minimum, you may think that you can chill for the rest of the time. These are just some of the very real reasons why Web3 companies place stringent policies upon your transparency in the workplace, and if your plan is to develop a flourishing, long-term career in this industry, you must abide by the transparency policies of the company hiring you.

What not a lot of employees in this industry think of is just how small this industry really is, and that at a certain level between company C-levels, they more or less all know each other, and if they don't, they can easily be connected just by asking around. For these reasons, not only would it be ethically bad for you to undermine their transparency protocol, but it would also be quite silly as it's virtually impossible to hide. Believe it or not, there's still a tremendous number of individuals that try, but seldom do they get away with it. The companies in this industry may sometimes seem overly protective and obsessed with transparency, but they really don't have any other choice...

Avoid Temptation

As you start to solidify your position within the Web3 company, you will be speaking to external entities such as clients, partners, service providers, market makers, and more. This is where you will, not maybe, but will be approached by some of them and persuaded to take lucrative bribes in exchange for helping them with more favorable commercial terms and conditions. You don't have to be in the sales team for this to happen either. You could be part of the business development team, a company lawyer, investment analyst, content creator, etc.... Every single person you will encounter will indeed try to obtain something from you. It may not even be to lower a price on a service they want; it may be to get better exposure, preferential terms, or to connect them with an important entity behind your company's back. All of these bribery attempts will come at you during the good times and the bad times. There may be moments where you feel that accepting $100,000 USD worth of their tokens may even be worth it, but remember, the transaction will take place on the blockchain and if you get caught, your contract will be terminated. There are also cases where the tokens people want to send you aren't a bribe, but simply to thank you for the hard work and effort you put into resolving a problem for them. This is where we enter the grey zone. Technically, you're not accepting a bribe; however, you are still receiving money that ethically should be going to the company employing you. If ever you find yourself in this situation, immediately reach out to your superior and inform them. This will be the absolute proof that you're transparent and the company will appreciate this show of ethics greatly. Depending on the company's decision, you may be able to either keep the entirety, a portion, or none of it. This can only be determined by the C-levels of the company you'll be in. If, on the other hand, you don't mention this and get caught, there are high chances your contract will be terminated immediately. Not only will you be out of a job without pay, your name will also be stained as such hearsay travels almost as fast as a transaction on the blockchain in this industry. Many people outside of your close circle will become aware of who you are and what you've done. Depending on the extent of damage done to your own brand, it may also become tortuous for you to find a new job and grow your career in this industry.

Multiple Jobs

A second point of transparency we mentioned in the opening paragraph of this chapter was working multiple jobs simultaneously. It may appear obvious, but it's inordinately taboo to work with more than one company in this industry. Even if your contract doesn't stipulate this, you can't work with more than one company at the same time. You may very well excel in your current job, but you still won't be allowed to do it. This all boils down to two reasons: time and insider leverage. Time, meaning that you should be so devoted to your current company that you spend every waking hour benefiting them. If you do have some extra time as you already hit your KPIs, the company expects that you naturally think outside of the box and lend a hand where needed. Insider leverage is the possibility that you will be using information, contacts, strategies, or any other form of intelligence belonging to your current company to benefit the second. Although that may not be the case, due to the number of amoral entities that do exist in this industry, your first company won't take the time to hear your side of the story, as the risk you were indeed doing insider leveraging is just too high. Once again, it's not a question of if you get caught; it's a question of when, and when you do get caught, your contract will be terminated instantly, sometimes without a heads up.

Staying Active

Finally, the last form of transparency is your daily activeness. As you'll be working remotely, the company won't have a physical presence watching over you. From day one, they'll be trusting you to fulfil your duties. As trust just isn't enough in the world of Web3, they will probably have daily check-ins for team members where your camera must be on, monitoring of your CRM, monitoring of your Telegram chats, and sometimes monitoring of your computer. Indeed, it is possible that they ask you to download a specific software that will monitor everything you're doing on your computer during company hours. Once again, depending on the company, they may not directly inform you about this, so to be on the safe side, always stay active. Don't get me wrong here; staying active doesn't mean just keep clicking on computer keys to make it look like you're doing something; it means actually working with direction. Working efficiently. At the end of the day, if you do take your job and missions seriously, you'll have plenty to do, so your monitored activity should be the least of your worries.

Transparency while working in a Web3 company is contemporaneous with trust. You'll be working in a highly volatile Wild West ecosystem where money talks. The company you'll work for is very much aware of this and that there will without a doubt be times where temptation will knock on your door. Never succumb to the bribes; work hard with direction and show respect to your company. Doing this will ensure longevity in your career, and by refusing bribes or monetary kickbacks from other companies, it will automatically prove to them that you're a trustworthy employee. You never know; maybe the individual asking if they should send a kickback to you or to your company may end up becoming your next boss!

Summary

As we can see, the main component revolving around working in this industry is to constantly perform. No matter the market conditions, sentiment, or time of year, you must always perform. In bad market conditions, the majority of crypto companies will make a portion of their workforce redundant during those times as they can't feed everyone through the crypto winter. The decisions on who goes and who stays are very much performance and value-based. Departments and roles can be prioritized, making some more prone to a higher percentage of layoffs than others. If you happen to be in a department that isn't a critical necessity but rather a luxury of the company, it doesn't mean that you will automatically be let go. Regardless of your role or department, if you surpass your KPIs, achieve your critical hits, and constantly strive to provide out-of-scope value to the company, you should be fine. In such scenarios, you may find yourself offered the option to take a completely different role in a more prioritized department as the workforce scales down into the core team. The only way you can ensure that you are indeed part of the core team is to constantly exceed expectations and targets while simultaneously bringing outside of the box added value to the company; moreover, make yourself as indispensable as possible to the company.

CHAPTER 11

How to Develop Your Crypto Career

Now that you've secured your job in crypto and are fully onboarded in Web3, it's time to take things to the next level. Generally speaking, and regardless of the work industry, may that be traditional corporate or crypto, no employee wants to be stuck in the same job position forever. You may call that human nature or simply ambition, but whatever the label you put on it, it's natural for your aspirations to grow as you evolve in the workspace. We see it very often in films or TV shows when a character has been made partner in a large law firm or is fighting for a promotion. The crypto industry is probably one of the fastest-growing sectors in the world as of now; hence, career growth is almost at the same pace. In just a couple of years, it is completely possible to become part of the C-suite if you play your cards right. Think of this entire industry as the old American dream. With a lot of hard work and dedication, you can make it to the top, just like what used to be possible in the corporate world of the United States. Now I'm not saying that the original American dream is dead, but it is far harder to accomplish the same growth and prosperity today than it was 50 years ago. The crypto realm is a simple reincarnation of that very essence. Low regulations with a heavily funded environment and a paroxysm of revolutionary start-ups from across the globe combined with a blank canvas create that same dynamic environment our ancestors were able to

© Alexander Rees-Evans 2024
A. Rees-Evans, *So You Want to Work in Crypto*,
https://doi.org/10.1007/979-8-8688-0503-5_11

benefit from in the golden years. In order to take full advantage of this new American dream, there's some strategic guidelines you can follow. That is why this very chapter is dedicated to doing just that!

Making Yourself Attractive

As we all know, the C-suite executives aren't on the front line, as they have more of a managerial role in the company. To evolve your career in this industry, among many other factors, you must also acquire and demonstrate the necessary skills put into practice by C-levels on a daily basis. You must also be mindful that even if career evolution in this industry can be remarkably fast, there are no shortcuts. You must still go through all of the necessary steps needed to get to the next level. If you aspire to become the Chief Business Development Officer (CBDO) of a launchpad but start as a junior business developer, you will have to work your way up through the ranks, such as evolving from that initial position to a business developer, then to your team leader, followed by the position of CBDO. It's extremely rare to jump from a junior position straight to a C-level position in a reasonably sized company in this industry. Subsequently, your first task when thinking of evolving your Web3 career is to identify those very steps, which job positions you need to move to and in which order. Depending on your job, role, company, and aspirations, these steps will vary heavily, so you will have to do some digging to put them under the spotlight.

Another component to identify for this part is whether the company you're in actually has the job position you wish to obtain and room for that growth. If you see that the same C-level positions have been occupied by the same individuals for a year or two, this can be interpreted in two ways. The first is that because the C-levels have been in position for so long, they themselves may be thinking about moving to the next level and evolving their career, so a spot may open up in the near future. On the other hand, it could also be interpreted as the C-levels have been there for such a long time that they plan to stay for even longer, making it harder for you to get to the C-suite as there will be no available openings. Once again, it's up to you to determine which one it is, and by asking some close teammates what they think of career evolution in the company, you can help paint you a more detailed picture of the potential of growth. When you've been able to fully assess the situation, you may find that there won't be potential to move to the C-suite, but there is a high possibility to be promoted to a higher position than you're currently in. This can also be very useful, as you'll be laying down the foundational blocks, helping you advance your career step by step.

Generally speaking, there is always some degree of potential career evolution in crypto companies. Once you've created the landscape of growth opportunities within your current company structure, there's another factor to be taken into account too; this is the reputational evolution. By means of direct engagement with larger Web3 companies, investors, projects, and service providers, you will automatically propel your career to the next level. The same may be said for the traditional corporate world. As an example, if you work as an account manager for a small local bank, you'll likely not engage with large influential clients. However, if you work as an account manager at Bank of America, even if you may not engage directly with large clients, your company does. By affiliating yourself with powerful and influential companies, your perceived value will automatically increase. You may even do less complex work than the account manager in the smaller local bank, but to the employer's eyes, the individual who worked at Bank of America will naturally be perceived as a more qualified employee. This may not be fair, and we may not like it, but it is the raw truth. Knowing this beforehand can help direct your career strategy in Web3 immensely, ensuring that you make it to the top. When planning your Web3 career strategy, it's important to take such factors as perceived value into consideration. In many cases, it is very hard to join a large influential company when you first join Web3, as they typically prefer seasoned industry veterans. For this reason, it's not uncommon for individuals to start their journey in a smaller Web3 company, and as they climb the ranks, they also upgrade to larger companies.

Either way, you will still have to evolve your skill set and industry knowledge in order to advance in this sector. Hereinafter, we'll now explore some of the key personal features you must enhance, thus preparing yourself for the next level.

Job Success

By far, the most important component to enhance is your current job performance. Without being successful in your immediate endeavor, it's not possible to be considered for promotion. Ensuring that your duty is fulfilled and KPIs always surpassed, you'll demonstrate to the leadership team that you're capable of performing highly in your primary role, hence potentially capable of uptaking more senior tasks.

Technical Skills

After proving to the company that you're capable of high performance on a constant basis, you'll need to acquire the technical skills for the next immediate job position. By asking colleagues who've been or are currently in a similar position you aspire to be in, you will start absorbing key pieces of information on what will be expected of you in such a role. Once you've understood this, it's time to start showing them off. In your day-to-day activities and especially in front of leadership, start acting on what you've learned. This could be demonstrating organizational skills, correcting important mistakes outside of your current role, or even demonstrating leadership qualities.

Industry Knowledge

Bulking up on industry knowledge is also a must to be suitable for promotions, as knowing the minimum just won't suffice. In your spare time, learn about deeper and more complex details in the blockchain space, such as how nodes (Glossary 39) work or other relevant industry complexities. Staying on top of current major events and trends is also important, as they can influence certain decisions a crypto company or its clients make, such as the launch of a major blockchain bringing more attention to the industry from retail investors; a major exchange collapse bringing the general market sentiment down; or the trend of a specific asset such as NFTs, meaning more focus on that area as there should be a lot of liquidity there. Being ahead of all of this will improve your efficiency and strategy when performing your daily tasks. During team meetings and when relevant, pointing out important events and how they could affect operations or clients can also impress the C-levels.

Finance and Economics

Before anything, this industry is deeply rooted in finance and economics. Understanding both of them is of grand necessity to evolve your career to the C-suite. Having a general sense of how global economies and financial markets work is intrinsically germane to comprehending the crypto market. Regularly studying the tokenomics of various projects will also provide you with industry insight into the general health and market conditions of the crypto realm too. Combining all of this information and understanding it will give you a large advantage over many other employees seeking promotions, as they seldom have such knowledge or comprehend the industry to that extent.

Communication

Humans have been communicating with each other for thousands of years, yet not a lot of individuals are effective communicators. Conveying your thoughts in a precise manner is essential to any company's well-being. Verbal communication is only one side of it, and by watching some YouTube videos on how to speak with power or reading some books on the matter can really help you improve. Secondly, it's the form of written communication where most of the misunderstandings happen. Your style, sophistication, and structure of writing will say a lot about you. A great book to help you improve on this is "The HBR guide to better business writing."

Sales

Regardless of your position, one of the most important skills any person can acquire is to sell. Think about it, how many times have you bought a product and it turned out to be a huge deception? The way it's packaged, phrased, or described plays a huge role in someone buying it. The same can be said about yourself. The way you present yourself, speak, and act determines the level of respect and confidence people give you, increasing or decreasing your general likability factor. By taking some sales courses or watching a few videos on how to sell, they will without a doubt teach you a few tricks on how to spin conversations and sway people to your side, making you an all-around more attractive person to work with.

The End Reward

Building up such traits can really enhance your profile in the Web3 sector. For sure, it requires a lot of personal work, time, and effort, but if you really want to evolve your career in this industry, there's no other way around it. Furthermore, a clear vision of what job you aspire to have when you reach the top will help your growth tremendously. This said, it can be very hard to know what end job you actually want as this industry moves so fast and is in a constant mode of growth. If you happen not to know what end position you want but still desire to grow your crypto career, it makes more sense to position your direction of growth towards companies rather than specific positions. Of course, you'll still have to be a high performer in a specific position with all of the qualities we've just been through, but instead of focusing on a specific career path to get a certain job, it's better to focus more on the operational side of things and work your way up to larger and larger companies until you work for one of the largest in the industry at a reasonably high level in a general operational position. This way, just like the example we cited earlier when comparing an account manager from a small local bank to an account manager from a larger bank such as Bank of America, you will have exceptional perceived value and should easily be able to adjust to a different role with enough credibility once you've made up your mind!

Value

Multiple times in this chapter, we've spoken about perceived value, but just what exactly does it mean? When talking about value, it's hard not to stray off onto a vague bridleway, slowly winding and turning without ever arriving at your destination. Value, one may argue, is subjective to whoever uses the term. For example, you may take great pleasure eating a plump, ripe cherry, whereas another individual may have a preference for an apple. The value of the two fruits is dependent on the individual on the receiving side. Due to this subjective angle, it's virtually impossible to determine the true value of an object or asset. Primarily, this is one of the reasons why fiat money is useful. It uses a monetary metric to define a specific value. Without this intermediate value between assets, we'd still be back in the days of barter and trading goat's milk for apples! Value can also have a very personal meaning too. A watch of a deceased loved one or a wedding ring passed on by generations, for many of us lucky enough to possess such an object, we wouldn't swap them even for a million dollars. In the workplace, much like the assets and objects we just touched upon, each employee has a certain value in the company. As we know, everyone's replaceable in the workplace; even if you're good at your job, there's always someone who can take your place the very next day. For this reason, you need to make yourself as hard as possible to replace by increasing your perceived value in the company.

I know we've said it a few times now and gave an analogy on perceived value; however, we must delve into what it means in your case. Perceived value is the esteem someone has for you by what they've seen or heard about you. This is why influencers, or Key Opinion Leaders (KOLs - Glossary 40), have so much traction with their communities. Often, and not just in the realm of crypto, you can see individuals with a very large social following they were able to build, selling products to them. With regard to perceived value, it's more so the individuals in crypto, trading, or any other area of expertise where they place themselves as experts to their followers. You can see them with multiple screens showing price charts and explaining why such a token will go up in price, and when and why you should buy it. They always act as if they're extremely talented in that domain and know more than you do. The fact of the matter is seldom are they experts, and they're just trying to promote a digital asset they have financial interest in. The worst part is that almost every time their community actually loses money rather than making money, yet, their communities almost always stick with them and repeat the same mistake time and time again. Among many reasons, one of the main ones is that they see so many other individuals following them, leading to the false idea that because so many people do follow them, they must know what they're doing and must be experts in that particular field.

Interestingly enough, a tremendous amount of individuals in this space do present themselves in such a manner that they come across as experts. The perception people have of them thanks to the way they dress themselves up is that of someone who knows what they're doing. In your case, there's no need to take it to this extreme; however, creating the perception that you are an expert in this field can be extremely positive for your career growth. Imagine if you show photos of yourself standing next to industry leaders on your Telegram account, or if you speak at a few large conferences in front of the entire crypto community. Automatically, individuals will perceive you as an expert or a veteran in the crypto industry, hence enhancing your status and credibility. Another option is to work on growing your social media presence, and just like KOLs, individuals will perceive you as someone of great status in this sector. For example, if you browse LinkedIn and see two individuals with the same roles in this space, working for different companies, one much larger than the other and one with 20,000 followers and the other with 300 followers, you will naturally come to the conclusion that the individual working in the more established company with 20,000 followers is much better at their job than the second person working in a small company with a smaller social following, just like the analogy with the account managers of the banks. Without a doubt in your mind, you will believe that the more visual individual is more competent and must be rather special to have accumulated such a large social following and work in a tier 1 company. Although the individual with the smaller perceived value may actually be a harder worker, smarter, and more efficient, the bottom line is nobody will take the time to think twice when comparing the two. In the eyes of a recruiter or employer, they will also come to the exact same conclusion, hence favoring the individual with a higher perceived value for promotions rather than the second choice.

As we know, perceived value doesn't necessarily mean that the visually smaller individual is less good at the same job; it just means that people perceive it that way. If you are looking to grow your career in crypto, you need to play along. There are, of course, many ways to increase your perceived value in this industry, and that's just what we're going to explore as of now. There are different categories of actions you can take to increase your perceived value, as follows:

1) Arguments of authority

   - Expert testimony: By citing your aligned views or ideas alongside those of established experts, your statement is automatically validated. If someone denies it, they're also denying those of a well-known expert.

   - Certifications: Having certifications from prestigious entities can also play a big part in your authority. If you pay for an online course from Harvard and obtain the diploma, you can say that you're Harvard-educated, further enhancing your credibility. Courses/diplomas in Web3 are also a value add.

   - Awards: By being given awards from reputable tier 1 companies in this industry, you will automatically be viewed as very knowledgeable of everything crypto, and someone denying that is also denying the credibility of the tier 1 company that gave you the award.

2) Public expertise

   - Publicly speaking: Speaking at a reputable conference or event in front of a public will without a doubt make you come across as an expert in your field. Everybody knows that if you publicly speak about a topic in front of a crowd, it's most likely because you've accumulated great expertise in that given area.

– Publishing content: Any content that you write on a particular topic will help solidify your status as an expert on that topic. By writing blogs, books, technical YouTube content, or articles on specific topics, you can drastically increase the perception the general public has of you and your industry expertise.

– Projects: Being part of a successful crypto project can immediately increase your perceived value in the eyes of the public. Just like Vitalik Buterin and Ethereum, the success of his token has propelled him on the world stage as one of the most knowledgeable experts in the industry.

3) Established affiliation

– Social media: By tagging along, commenting, and sharing established content, but more importantly, trying to get a very well-established individual to like, share, or comment on one of your posts can lead to an exceptional boost in your visibility and credibility.

– Physical presence: As goes the old saying, "Show me your friends and I'll show you your future," if you're lucky enough to travel to crypto events, try to connect with industry leaders and KOLs. After some of them see you regularly enough, at future conferences or events they'll naturally speak to you. The surrounding attendees will witness this and instinctively think that you must be of importance.

- Brands: If you're lucky enough to have some hefty funds at your disposal, you can also buy your way in. One of the largest financial brands globally will not only feature you in an article for the right price but can grant you an esteemed title; of course we're talking about Forbes. It is completely possible to buy your way in Forbes 30 under 30 or other categories, creating a powerful aura around you.

4) Mentoring

- Companies: Becoming a mentor in programs of prestigious entities will undeniably prove that you are an expert. Joining a prestigious program as a mentor can be quite the challenge, as you need to create a relationship with the individuals running it. The time spent doing this will without a doubt always be a step in the right direction for your perceived value.

- Projects: Mentoring a project founder or team isn't quite the same as advising due to the fact that, generally speaking, mentors aren't paid, whereas for advisors they are. Mentoring is usually the transmission of information from a highly experienced individual to a less experienced but highly motivated individual.

5) Government affiliations

- Regulations: Arguably not one of the easiest positions to obtain, helping a government or state on their crypto regulations is by far one of the most impressive forms of service you can provide. You do, however, have to be heavily experienced and well connected to even think of doing this, but it's still a possibility.

- Blockchain advice: As we saw the eNaira, the failed digital currency of Nigeria, advisors for governments can't just have perceived value with a few high-level connections. If you do go down this road, be sure that you're capable of delivering, and if you do, you can easily claim to be one of the world's best experts in this industry.

6) Leadership roles

- Assistance leadership: Acting as the right hand of a C-level for managing and accomplishing tasks can be a great way to show them your leadership skills and that you are indeed capable of taking on and fulfilling such a duty long term.

- Team leadership: Becoming the leader of your team is one of the most rewarding positions you can accept. When this happens, your leadership style will instantly be put to the test as you're trying to get your friends to work and hit deadlines. This is where you will have to set in boundaries and make the new relationship dynamic work. If you're successful, once again the C-levels will be impressed.

7) Trust

- Work fulfilment: As we know, this entire industry is still based on a lot of trust. Your employer will have to trust you to actually do the work behind your screen, and there's nobody behind you to make sure you've done it. By doing a great job day in and day out, you will show the C-levels that they can trust you to work.

- Ethics: As your career in Web3 evolves, you will inevitably be offered bribes in exchange for more favorable conditions for a client or partner. Saying no is a very important step as on top of the ethics side, that very person may simply be testing you, or could even be your next boss!

- Transparency: If you make a mistake, own it. Don't beat around the bush; simply own it. By being so straightforward and humble about a mishap, you can only receive respect from your peers. A zero-ego mindset and full accountability behavior will slowly forge your persona to that of a champion, one who constantly evolves.

For there are many more forms of value you can state that would potentially increase your perceived value; the ones cited above are however the most important. If you're able to work on all seven of these value categories, you will grow your career in this industry. All of this will take some time and passion, but if you're certain that this industry is for you and wish to make the most out of it, just like the prior segment, there are some steps you can't skip. Building your value up in this industry isn't easy; if it was, everyone would do it. It is, however, possible and fast-tracked compared to the traditional corporate world. By sticking to a solid plan to grow your career and following the steps to grow your perceived value, you will inevitably grow your own experience and knowledge base too. Intrinsically, by focusing on the seven value categories, you will gain in perceived value, but you will also grow in value you can provide to clients, partners, and collaborators!

In order to actually grow your own work value alongside your perceived value, you can't just focus on one or two of the seven points. You need to work on as many of them as possible to strengthen your knowledge base and enhance your understanding of the industry. There's no need to work on all of the points simultaneously if you're already busy fulfilling the duties in your current job, but you can focus on a bunch of them when you go to conferences, for example, during team meetings or during the evening before you go to bed. However you follow through on your organization, be sure to absorb as much new information as possible so you don't just affiliate, you assimilate.

Network

So far, we've explored some of the main points on how to make yourself attractive in the marketplace and how to elevate your perceived value. We covered almost every single aspect apart from a final, key metric. The component we're about to discuss may even supersede in importance the above topics; we're talking here about your network. The old adage "Your network is your net worth" may be one of the most accurate statements ever made, and this for multiple reasons. You may have increased your perceived value, learned the tricks of the trade, or even become capable of fulfilling your duty in a superior job position, but you'll never make it to the very top without having a stellar network. One of the most valuable qualities you can bring to the table, and this regardless of your role, is a tier 1 network. Why you may ask? Simply because working in a tier 1 company in a tier 1 position requires you to bring tier 1 value adds. A very interesting note here is that it's who you know that determines to some extent what you're capable of achieving, not just for yourself, but for the company hiring you. Your network can carry you a very long way in this industry whilst also making your life far easier. When your company can count on you to make important introductions that will benefit them financially, strategically, or efficiency-wise, you start to provide another level of value to them. When you're able to reach this level of value add to a company, you will automatically be given a more senior position, a higher salary, more responsibility, and finally be part of the C-suite. In this final segment, we'll discuss how to develop such a network and how you can use it to not just the company's advantage but also your own.

Firstly, you must note that building a network is a natural sign of positive evolution in your crypto career. If you spend a few years in this industry and aren't able to develop a strong network, most likely you're doing something wrong and won't progress to a C-suite position in a tier 1 company, no matter how good you become in your profession. There are, of course, some exceptions, such as developers or accountants, where your network really isn't that relevant. For almost all of the other jobs in this industry, you need to grow a powerful and reliable one. Having a first-class network is completely useless if the people in it don't reply to you when they need you, and having a second-class network is completely useless when you're trying to make it to the big league. This isn't to say that starting from day one you need to befriend the head of tokenomics of Binance, but it is to say that such relationships should be your goal as you evolve in this sector. Building relationships with tier 1 entities is one of the hardest challenges you will face during your career in crypto. Reason being, every single individual in this industry wants to speak to them too. For example, if you wish to become the head of partnerships at the Solana foundation, you're going to need to bring much more to the table than just some connections with media companies and exchanges. If you wish to become the head of sponsorships at Kraken, you'll need to have exceptional connections with extraordinarily large companies in both Web2 and Web3. If you wish to be the head of the legal department of a 16z, you'll more than likely be expected to have relations with governments and their regulatory bodies. Regardless of your role in Web3, in order to get to the very top, you need to build up a stellar network aligned with your field.

It is also possible to be somewhat of a generalist in this art too. If you've worked on the front line in a very large crypto media company directly engaging with all of the clients, it's completely possible to develop a prodigious network. Often, just by having such relationships can open new job opportunities in fields you would have never imagined just because you're able to connect the dots at a high level. Having a powerful network doesn't only bring value to the company you'll work for by making important connections and driving their business forward; it's proven to be extremely important for yourself too. Among many, we'll touch upon two of the ways that having such a network can benefit you: networks and opportunities.

Growing Your Business

By owning a very special network, it can open job avenues you may not have originally considered or even thought of! Many crypto companies looking to grow their business and take it to the next level are in dire need of such capital connections. Without an individual with such an existing network onboard, the company itself will have to spend the time and money on one or two of their team members to go out and try to build it from scratch. This means paying for flights, hotels, conference tickets, restaurants, nights out, and champagne bottles if required, among other company expenses. Furthermore, doing all of this doesn't guarantee results, and it can take quite some time repeating the same process to develop and then nurture just one of these relationships until the company's able to start trying to do business with that individual or entity. In hindsight, it's completely absurd to indulge in such exotic expenses just to get, at best, a small handful of important connections when the company can simply hire one individual for maybe $10,000 USD per month who already has ten times those connections. In this case, it really is a win for both the employer and the employee, as the company will be saving time, money, and guaranteeing results, whereas the employee can find themselves making a very comfortable living in exchange for providing their network.

Opportunities

The other side of the coin is that as you develop your network, you will most likely come across new opportunities. Opportunities in this sector are plentiful if you know where to look, and when engaging with high quality relations, the more high-quality opportunities will appear. The first obvious opportunity is a job offer, and a lot of the job offers in this space get filled by word-of-mouth. The fact of the matter is that as you develop your network into one of a grander stature, you will automatically come across C-levels from different companies in the industry. If you make a good impression, it's likely that they'll make you an offer on the spot, as talent in Web3 is hard to come by. If it doesn't happen instantly, they may offer you a position a few months down the line when they have an opening. It's all about timing, demonstrating your skills, and building trust.

On the more company-related subjects, your network is vital to providing added value to the company and really making a difference. To become a C-level, on top of being extremely capable and knowledgeable, you have to be able to propel the company to never-before-achieved heights. This is why the following sections will explain how to develop a tier 1 network.

Conferences and Events

Attending renowned conferences such as Token 2049, Paris Blockchain Week, Consensus, or ETHCC can be great places to bump into tier 1 entities where you can directly engage with them. A useful trick here is to be at the conference or event as early as possible; it's not uncommon to see the more senior individuals visit at early hours. That's not to say they don't attend the event during daytime, but you'll by far increase your chances of being able to sit down with them and have a real discussion during the opening hours. A simple explanation for this is that there will be far less attendees trying to approach them, as there will be far less attendees early in the morning. Getting into the hottest side events is a must also. If you've managed to have a good discussion with a person of interest earlier on at the conference, meeting them again in a more relaxed setting with a few drinks can definitely help create a tight, memorable bond. You must keep in mind that many people will try to approach and create a bond with the same important people over the conference period. For this reason, you need to make sure that your bond will last the most. Always remember, people do business with people, not companies.

Groups and Associations

Affiliating yourself with prestigious groups and/or associations is yet another, very powerful way of developing your network. If you have the possibility to attend physical meetings, it can be a great way to strengthen ties with individuals you've communicated with over the computer and create new relationships with others. The quality of the individuals in the given association or group will be completely dependent on how exclusive they are. Usually speaking, there are much more accessible groups you can enter with ease and start building up your network prior to joining an established association such as the World Business Union or the European Blockchain Association. You can often find some easy-access groups on Telegram, but you must be careful not to communicate thoughtlessly in these private groups, as you can get kicked out of them if the moderators determine you're a nuisance. Once you've grown your network through such groups, try to do good business with the individuals you've connected with. This is how you'll be able to solidify that relationship and expand your network.

Social Media

As we've discussed earlier in this chapter, your perceived value is important, and one of the outlets for this is LinkedIn. Having a polished LinkedIn profile with thousands of connections doesn't just look good;

it can reveal to be of extreme utility for your networking too. By browsing key words through the search bar, you can connect with some of the most influential people in this industry. Although the connection will be futile to begin as it's not a warm introduction, if you're able to craft a seductive enough message, the individual should reply. If you make it to that stage, try to organize a video conference with them to introduce yourself formally. After that, you have to prove yourself business-wise to solidify and then grow the relationship. This may not be the most dynamic platform for serious networking, but it does boast the potential to contact almost every important person from the crypto industry with a simple click of a button.

Referrals

This is one of the most powerful forms of networking in existence to date. A warm introduction is the best start to a relationship you could wish for. From the very start, both parties trust each other thanks to the mutual friend. Cutting through all of the red tape at the beginning will save you a lot of time and effort, as the most important factor is already existent: trust. A great way to leverage your referrals is to try and keep an ascending trend for each one. This isn't to say that the second you're introduced to an individual, ask that newly befriended person for an introduction to someone else straight away, as that simply would not work and would probably end in damaging your newly found relationship more than anything. It's wise to wait a minimum of ten days for a referral from a newly found relation. This ten-day delta is only valid, however, if you really build a great relationship with them and fast. If you feel that the relationship isn't there, give it some more time and effort prior to asking for an introduction to someone.

In conclusion, your network is by far the only asset capable of advancing people to the next level, even if that person doesn't have the skill set to fulfil their duties correctly. In the traditional world, we see this all of the time, people getting hired in the local mayor's office because their mother is a friend of the mayor's wife, politicians hiring family members as staff, or CEOs of companies hiring their close friends to help run the business. Without discussing ethics, I think we can all agree that we all know or have heard of someone getting a job for a similar reason, not because of their qualifications or capabilities on the job. All of this, while someone who's genuinely qualified with tremendous skill, doesn't get the job because they didn't know the right person at the right time. With this context, a question may be generated as follows: "For whom is the most intelligent? He who spent years perfecting their craft, or he who didn't, yet got the job within one week because they knew the right person?" If we're talking about efficiency, it is without a doubt he who knew someone. It may not be fair; you may not like it, but either way, it's the brutal yet honest truth. It goes without saying that you need to have the skills to do the job too, so you may keep it, then master your job, increase your perceived value, and develop your network simultaneously. Once you've found the perfect balance between being mighty good at your job and owning a first-class network, don't be shy to leverage your network when exploring new job positions, as knowing the right people at the right time can be life-changing.

Summary

In traditional jobs, many a time employees get stuck on the corporate ladder; this is also a possibility in the field of crypto. This isn't, however, to say that it happens at the same ratio or scale as it does in the traditional corporate environment; it's more so that individuals get lost in choice, don't excel fast enough, or simply don't grow. Now if you're satisfied with a specific job position and want to keep it for the next 20 years, the chances that it will happen are extremely slim due to the ever-changing landscape of crypto. Trends, regulations, market conditions, and constantly fluctuating conditions mean that companies can incur problems and have to downsize their teams overnight. If you really wish to thrive in this industry, you have to be constantly evolving. By perpetually growing professionally, you will automatically outgrow certain positions and companies; by the very nature of this concept, you will automatically be required to gain in hierarchy, making yourself less and less disposable, or move to a larger company where you will have more opportunity to grow. Working in Web3 requires you to keep moving and to always keep growing; this undeniable concept is paramount to keeping a job; in short, it's an eat or be eaten mindset. If you don't keep this growth mindset, eventually something will happen to either yourself, your position, or the company. Keep sharp, keep growing, and keep hungry.

CHAPTER 12

Words of Wisdom

In the final chapter of this book, and in your best interest, I decided to delve deep into some key, core factors of this industry that are far too often overlooked or brushed upon lightly. Sharing wisdom is the art of transferring knowledge and tips from a more experienced individual to a less experienced individual. Wisdom is one of the most important gifts anyone could wish for, regardless of the sector or role. With such a gift, you save time and energy and get things done right almost immediately in the most efficient of ways, thanks to the knowledge and tips shared with you. Without such backing, you have to learn the tricks of the trade and figure everything out by yourself. This entire book is designed to transfer as much industry wisdom as possible to you without having to leave your living room. One very interesting piece of wisdom here is that of how to conduct yourself in the Web3 space.

Ethics and Deontology

In this segment, we'll delve deeply into some of the most overlooked and underappreciated traits you could possibly have in Web3. Among these forgotten ones, we have two components that will remain with you constantly during your time in the crypto workforce, whether you try to shake them off or not. We're now going to discuss two of the most underrated characteristics all employees should have and all employers value: ethics and deontology in the crypto workplace.

© Alexander Rees-Evans 2024
A. Rees-Evans, *So You Want to Work in Crypto*,
https://doi.org/10.1007/979-8-8688-0503-5_12

Ethics

I'm highly confident that you're familiar with ethics, and we can both agree that different people have different standards of them. There is however a common sense across the board of what's ethical and what isn't, regardless of the situation. We all know that it's ethically right to give your seat to a pregnant woman on the bus, although it doesn't mean that everybody does it, even if it is the ethical thing to do. This very same principle can be applied to the world of crypto, but on a much larger and riskier scale. An ethical code of conduct in this industry varies from company to company, but generally speaking, there are a few parameters of which remain unchanged that we'll now look into.

Trust and Reliability

Due to the decentralized nature and unique operational format of working in crypto, many employers and companies will have to trust you. This isn't just about trusting you to do your job; it's trusting you to do a good job. The multiple time zones, cultures, and people in this industry mean that the industry never sleeps. Weekdays, weekends, holidays, there's always a large amount of people working in this industry around the clock to keep driving it forward. Whether you're an American who celebrates Thanksgiving, a European hoping to take time off for Christmas, a Muslim awaiting Zakat, or a person of Jewish heritage looking to take some time off for Yom Kippur, there will always be others working during those periods. A big part of working in Web3 is being available constantly; however, it's not to say that you can't take time off, it's simply to emphasize that you can never disconnect completely. By making yourself, to some degree, always available, including weekends, evenings, and during your vacations, you will build immense reliability, and your company will undeniably trust you.

Behavioral Management

Any and all companies that will hire you will have standards they're looking to either build, grow, or maintain. When they hire you, you must keep that in mind at all times. They're of course hiring you to fulfil a specific duty, and we've been through the particular intricacies, something like that beholds, but their reputation is another major factor to be considered. Imagine that you're extremely good at your job, but you get into a heated argument with an important partner or client and lose your cool. That very same partner can spread negative hearsay about your company, hence leading to reputational damage and a decline in profits. This industry is still really quite small, and between all of the well-known figures of the space, word-to-mouth travels extremely fast. You must control yourself at all times, whether you're right or wrong; if not, regardless of how good at your job you are, they will most likely fire you. Once you've been let go for such a reason, depending on the amplitude of the situation, future employers may hesitate before hiring you too. All in all, keeping the standards of the company in mind at all times will not only help them, but will also help you.

Tier 1 Growth

Earlier in this book, we understood that tier 1 essentially means top of their class. As you do start to grow in Web3, your company will likely start to trust you with larger and more high-tier contacts. You may be a lawyer, account manager, marketeer, or even on the sales side; either way, the more you'll grow, the more your contacts will too. This of course is a good thing; however, when your company entrusts you with such contacts, you cannot afford to make mistakes. You must start to grow on a personal level also to ensure that you match the quality of the entities you'll be engaging with. The way you hold and present yourself must evolve alongside your skills, knowledge, and perceived value also. Every time you receive a higher tier of clients, make sure that you match their level.

Deontology

As for deontology, there are similar guidelines you'll need to follow. The term deontology is derived from the Greek deon, "duty," and logos, "science." In the Web3 space, it is often aligned with your ethics, but on top of your ethics, you must place the well-being of the company at the very heart of all decisions you'll make. As an example, let's say that you become a trading analyst in a major CEX and obtain inside information that will prove to be very lucrative if leveraged in a trading activity. If you wish to maintain a high standard of deontology, you will not use this information to your advantage. Insider trading is just one of the many sectors where your deontology in the Web3 space may be tested. Think of it like politicians when they have absurd net worths but when compared to their annual salaries, it just doesn't add up. A prime example of this is Nancy Pelosi out of the United States. According to the news outlet International Business Times, as of now, and at the peak of her career, she boasts an annual salary of approx. $223,000 USD, yet she has a net worth of over $170,000,000 USD! Although there's no tangible proof of insider trading, it's rather obvious as to what is going on, hence why her deontology standards are often questioned (US Congress Salaries 2022: How Much Does Nancy Pelosi, Other Reps. Earn? | IBTimes). When you're placed in a position of power in this sector, you need to uphold your standards and always keep in mind a strong conviction of honorable righteousness in your day-to-day endeavors. To provide some more substance, the following sections will elaborate on some other points of deontology.

Consistency

Indeed, deontology is also how you treat and act with regard to your company's goals and ambitions. Consistency is one of the hardest traits to find in any employee and can also be a trigger for promotion. Upholding the same standards day in and day out is a great way to show that you care about the company and have its best interests at heart. Doing the opposite, showing highly fluctuating results and work intensity, can be a red flag to many employers, as they don't think that you're fully dedicated to the job, nor do you care about the company. Make sure that you show consistency on a daily basis, and remember, working in this industry isn't a sprint; even if you may get that impression, it's a high-paced marathon.

Preventing Ethical Breaches

Depending on the company that you'll work for, they may ask every employee to report any wrongdoings or actions to a designated person in the company. In short, they may ask you to inform them if you see or hear of any suspicious activity from your colleagues. This may include insider trading, accepting bribes, stealing company funds, or working more than one job simultaneously. Often, there will be a conflict between your personal relationship with the specific colleague and the company's interests. It can be quite challenging to hold an impartial, almost robotic form of conduct in these cases, so it will almost always come down to your own judgement and depth of deontology.

Respecting Rights

In almost every possible job position available in the crypto sector, you will almost certainly find yourself at one time or another handling sensitive client and/or company information. Safeguarding such information is paramount to withholding a high deontological standard. You may find yourself in front of the contact information of a celebrity looking to launch their NFT collection, never-before-released music content from a world famous artist, or simply confidential information obtained after signing a Non-Disclosure Agreement (NDA - Glossary 41). Regardless of the temptation, you must abide by company policy and/or guidelines and what information you may or may not share. No matter how much you wish to impress your friends or family, only disclose what you're allowed to.

Finding a harmonious balance between your ethics, deontology, and the many diverse scenarios you will face in Web3 will be of grand importance for your evolution and genuine enjoyment of working in this sector. You will face moments filled with challenges and temptation, or simply situations where you just aren't sure. When this happens, whenever you're in doubt, don't hesitate in reaching out to your hierarchy or colleagues to seek guidance. Asking such questions will reassure the company executives that you undoubtedly have the company's interest at heart and are trustworthy and honest. On the other hand, if you're not sure of a situation and make the wrong decision and the C-levels do find out, regardless of your intentions, it can lead to a direct termination. If ever you're in doubt, simply ask around and explain to them why you're asking, stating that from an ethical and deontological perspective, you're not quite sure about how to react to something that can only be beneficial. This way, the C-levels know that you do indeed have high ethical and deontological standards, and regardless of the situation, will be far more inclined to trust you.

Reputation

A reputation can take years to build but only needs seconds to be destroyed. Across the board, reputation is one of the most powerful tools you can add to your arsenal. By mere hearsay, it's possible to destabilize clients, win contracts, or impress colleagues and other Web3 companies. Having a well-established and credible reputation in the Web3 space will dramatically improve your perceived value but also your credibility. Companies, brands, and individuals have their own respective reputations, be they good or bad. Even countries have reputations for certain things, such as France for gastronomy and fashion, Germany for engineering, or China for cost-efficient products. Some may call these "stereotypes," but at the end of the day, the type and quality of services or products you deliver will eventually become known for something that characterizes them. Every single time you engage with an individual or entity in this space, the manner in which you proceed will over time create a memorable pattern. This pattern will, in its turn, become your trademark of quality. It can be cross-referenced between entities, expanded to such a degree that all become aware of it, up to the point where your pattern becomes so stable and high-quality that entities all around the world want to work with you because of your reputation.

There are many forms and ways that a reputation may be built, and even more that they may be destroyed. In our case, it's important to note that the reputation you'll want to build is that of extremely high quality in regard to your network in the industry and capacity to deliver. Needless to say that in the last chapter we discussed how to develop your network and deliver on what you promise is a given, so as of now, we'll focus more on the global aspect of building a reputation. Now reputations can take a lot of time to build, and before you start, you need to make sure that you can also deliver. Once you're confident enough in your skill set, you can focus on building up your reputation, and one of the best ways to start is by placing yourself alongside tier 0 and tier 1 entities in this space. Just like that old saying, "You are what you eat," here, you are who you hang around with. Somewhat like the cool kids back in school, the individuals part of that small group automatically became cool by association. Here you need to do a little bit more than just hang around with very reputable entities, but it still somewhat follows the same logic.

There's a very fine line between perceived value and reputation; in the case of the cool kids, the perceived value of them all being cool exists; however, if the whole class keeps speaking about just one of them and shares stories on why they're cool, suddenly they have a strong reputation of being it. On the other hand, if you stay in that class for a year and constantly see one other group member just tagging along and not having any stories being told on why they're cool, their perceived value declines, hence their reputation. Perceived value and reputation are intertwined to some extent, but reputation is the direct result of maintaining your perceived value for some time. As we know, there are both positive and negative forms of perceived value; for instance, if you join a very small, low-quality tier 3 crypto company, you will naturally be associated with the same level of quality (perceived value). If you stay there for years, you will build a reputation resembling that of a low-quality, tier 3 individual (reputation). There's no exact science as to the time it takes for your perceived value to transform into your reputation, but the entities of which you surround yourself with do influence this heavily.

As we've agreed earlier in this book, it's virtually impossible to work for a high-tier crypto company when you first start, so you do need to start at a lower-tier company, hence with a lower quality reputation in many cases. This is where you need to work your way up strategically, and we'll get into that very shortly, but for now, we're going to explore how you can correctly transform your perceived value into a long-lasting reputation once on the right track.

Honoring Your Word

We all agree that loyalty is highly valued in this sector, and keeping to your word is the next level. If you say to a colleague, partner, or client that you will do x for 15h00mins CET Friday, make sure it's done. Not meeting your promised deadlines can really provoke a deception in the minds of those you've not delivered to on time. Small mistakes like this can leave big lasting impressions, for better or for worse. It's always good to give yourself a security timeline by adding an extra hour, day, or week to whatever deadline you will give. It's far easier this way to always impress when you deliver, as it will almost always be before the end of the deadline. The same goes for any introductions or tasks you state that you'll do, no matter how futile they may be. Always make sure that you honor your word by following through in a timely manner.

Being Present

Making yourself constantly present for clients or colleagues is also a very big component to building up your reputation. That said, making yourself present doesn't necessarily mean that you have to take a call at 03h00mins in the morning; it simply means that if a client or colleague sends you a message after working hours, you reply. Simply responding and exchanging a few messages late at night or early in the morning can make all the difference and give your counterpart a real impression that you're there for them. Just one message stating that a particular point is noted and will be resolved first thing the next morning will be appreciated. You must never leave messages pending and always try to reply within the hour every single time. This will drastically solidify all relationships with clients and colleagues alike. By keeping this iron mentality during your entire crypto career, you will soon set yourself apart from other individuals and build a reputation of always being available and ready for business no matter the day or the hour. This mentality is really appreciated by both clients and C-levels of all companies in this industry.

Feedback

Asking for feedback from colleagues and C-levels is also a great way to constantly grow and improve yourself. Nobody knows everything, no matter how smart or experienced they are, and one of the best ways to improve a skill is to always ask what you could do better. If you're good at a particular skill and ask colleagues this question, at first they will tell you that there's nothing to improve and you're great. I guarantee you that if you push a second, third, and then fourth time, they will come up with a small, minute detail that you can improve. Asking for feedback after handling a client's complaint, pitching to investors, drafting a contract, or speaking on a podcast, among other scenarios, is the only way you can actually improve your skill set. If you ask for such feedback after every client call, you can only get better. Doing this will of course improve your skills and talent, but it will also come across as a powerful growth mindset, which will soon become engraved in their minds. Someone who never stops growing and is always improving. This is one of the most dangerous mindsets an individual can have in a highly capitalist environment such as Web3, and with it, you will get to the top and be known as an unstoppable force.

Consistency

As said by the great Eric Thomas, "Practice doesn't make perfect, practice makes permanent." In order to move your perceived value to a solidified status of reputation, you need to make your perceived value permanent. When you've found your ideal perceived value, you need to repeat, repeat, and repeat until the features of your perceived value become second nature traits that define you. Consistency in your method is key to preserving the standards you uphold, quality provided, and pattern you install. Without this repetition leading to consistency, you may very well find yourself with fluctuating perceived value, which over a period of time will become the pattern that defines you, and you don't want this to be the case. In all cases, you must create a stable environment for your perceived value to flourish and keep it up over a long enough period of time until your perceived value is permanent, thus creating your reputation.

There are many other ways you can develop a reputation, but leading with a high perceived value then maintaining it for a protracted period is the most certain way of doing this. Again, that's not to say that this is the only way, but by far this will provide you with a tangible method helping guide you as you're building your reputation in this industry. Without a doubt, you need to keep all of your decisions from day one aligned with this vision to create a preordained foundation for your future reputation. As soon as you've started to solidify your perceived value and transform it into your newly developed reputation, the next step is to amplify it. Having a reputation in a small, close circle is good, but it can only carry you so far. If your goal is to have an almost globally recognized reputation, you can't afford to stay in small circles.

Much like a product when being taken to market, you need to reach as many people as possible. You may build the next generation of maritime propulsion, superseding all other forms, but if only you and a handful of individuals know about it, the chances are the product will never sell enough to be sustainable. It goes without saying that if only yourself and the five largest maritime propulsion suppliers in the world know about your product, it should sell just fine, but the chances are your small circle won't be filled with the industry's largest clients in need of your services. This is something you need to aspire to once you have created your reputation, but to get there, you need your reputation to scale. Without adequate scaling of your reputation, you can soon find yourself stuck with the same tier of clients or companies surrounding you, and, after a while of staying in that environment, even if they're high tier 2 entities and maybe some tier 1, your reputation will once again become that of a tier 2/tier 1 employee. Now there's nothing wrong with this, and if you're happy with that, you can stay at that level and take things easy. If on the other hand, you want to be part of the elite and climb to the top of this industry, you need to scale your reputation.

The next two sections provide some useful tips on scaling your reputation that will help you along the way.

Social Media

Leveraging powerful social media platforms to your advantage can prove to be extremely efficient for spreading awareness about a particular subject. Furthermore, you don't have to be a marketing wizard to do this either; you can very easily hire a social media manager to do this for you, and the great part is that you can pay the majority of them in crypto! Once you reach this stage in your career, you need to start investing in your own personal brand, and if you've done everything correctly, you should be on a fairly decent pay. With the extra funds at your disposal, you can start to hire a social media manager to do a few posts per week across all of your main social media accounts, including X (formally Twitter) and LinkedIn. This way, your own brand awareness and following will start to grow, enabling your social media manager to share carefully crafted content relevant to enhancing and sharing your reputation with the world.

Crypto Media

Befriending editors and journalists from tier 1 crypto news outlets is a great way to start getting media coverage also. Crypto news outlets can charge ridiculous amounts of money to publish an article under their name, and the goal isn't to break the bank either. Even if you're making $20,000 USD a month, it's a shame to spend $100,000 USD on a media package... Media companies in Web3 can be extremely expensive, but there are other ways around this. Tier 1 crypto news outlets are always looking for big, never-before-heard of stories or content for articles. By doing this, they provide fascinating content to their readers and keep them hooked on their brand. Just like CEXs, crypto news outlets and media companies are almost only interested in user/reader acquisition. Without their users/readers, their entire business model collapses. For this reason, tier 1 media companies and news outlets will publish content for free if it's juicy enough and you know the right people. Once you've befriended an editor, all you have to do is ask what stories, topics, or content they're interested in at that moment in time and tie yourself in the loop. Try to fit yourself in the picture by making yourself part of such a story they're looking to publish thanks to your expert insight, alpha news, or simply by helping them out.

On top of potentially getting some Key Opinion Leaders (KOLs) (the social media influencers in Web3 that promote digital assets to their communities such as IBC, Dingaling, Tarik Bilen, Crypto Banter, or even Batman), who could potentially post about your successes if they're are open to this, but seldom will they do it for free or placing client testimonials on your own personal website, one of the most efficient ways of spreading your reputation is through social media and crypto media. Undeniably, they're the most scalable tools any entity should use to obtain hyper visibility in this space. You must, however, remember that once you start projecting your reputation for the entire industry to see, there's no going back. You can't change or tweak your reputation after it's left your small circle, so when you do enter this phase, be sure that the reputation you're about to take public is the reputation you're happy with. If you feel that it could be better, then you need to take the time to modify your perceived value, then stabilize it long enough for it to become your reputation. Once you're happy with your reputation, you can go ahead and take it mainstream, but whatever you do, don't rush it because once it's live, there's no going back.

Roadmap

Now that you have a clear, helicopter view of what needs to happen, write it down and integrate yearly goals to help keep you on track, manifestation works. Use it to progress your career in Web3; paint a clear roadmap of what you should do and when in order to have a stellar career in this industry. By going faster than the music and trying to do everything at once, you can't possibly do everything right. From your very first interview to job choices, industry knowledge, complex market cycles, and work mentality all the way up to your perceived value and reputation, you need to put in place a vision. This doesn't mean that you have to know what job and company you want to work for five years from now; this simply means that you want to prepare a trajectory, leading you to the tier 1 realm. Regardless of your initial level, job, or qualifications, in this industry, you can make it big time, but the only way to achieve that is by always aiming high. Creating a generic roadmap of strategic steps that you need to take from day one will provide you with a positive trajectory, helping you stay on track. Another interesting way to use this roadmap is by actually making a physical one that you can update as you go along. This way, you will have a visual on the evolution of your career in this space, making it very obvious when you're not going in the right direction or need help making a strategic decision. Think of your career in Web3 as a brand new business. When a new business starts, they have a goal and a use case they leverage to obtain that goal; however, as the business takes off, almost every aspect of it will need to be modified as they go along because nobody knows what the future holds. The only element keeping a newly formed business on track is the end vision of the founding members. In our case, the end vision, the ultimate goal, is to climb to the very top of the crypto ladder, start changing the world, and have the best possible career you can imagine!

It goes without saying that first and foremost you need to get your foot through the door, so don't be too fussy about what company you'll work for at the very beginning. The advantage of doing this is that it will provide you with enough time to become acquainted with the industry and how it all works. Even if you manage to get a job in a well-established company, the danger is that you won't be able to keep up with the pace, so in many cases, this can backfire. Think of your first job in the industry as your learning ground. You must, however, always keep in mind that just because they're not a large, well-known company, that doesn't mean that they won't hesitate to fire you if you're not productive. Make sure that you really do try your hardest to stay on top of everything, even if it will primarily serve as your training ground. Once you've landed your first job in this space, it's time to start following your roadmap and evolving your career. The main action you need to take when aspiring to evolve in this industry is to always be on the move. You can't afford to stay in one place for too long until you've reached the top, and even then it's still constantly pushing to stay there. In this final segment, we'll discuss timelines for each stage of your journey in this space, ensuring that you're fully equipped from A-Z to not only make the most but also offer the most to this wonderful space.

First Job: 3–6 Months

Your first job is important for you to become fully immersed in this space, learn important crypto knowledge, understand how the ecosystem works to a certain degree, and pick up positive habits. As we said during the opening remarks of this book, it's highly unlikely that you'll land a tier 1 job when you start off, so you need to settle for a smaller tier company. Now if a company isn't tier 1, it's for many reasons, all of which aren't necessarily bad. It could be that they've just started off, they want to stay in their niche, or even that they just don't have the right people onboard to propel them to the next level, although they provide great services. It's simply just not the same as if the founders were terribly incompetent or that their services were abysmal. Regardless, you will be familiarized with the industry within your first few months working in the crypto space, so you need to move as fast as possible to a higher-tier company. The goal was never to have a career in your first company, and you shouldn't feel bad about changing companies, because they won't hesitate to change you if you don't live up to expectations. Absorb everything you can from them and start applying for similar roles in a higher-quality company. Also, it may seem very unusual to join a company then leave a few months later, but once again, this is an extremely fast-paced environment so it's quite normal.

Second Job: 1–2 Years

Now that you've joined a higher tier company, you can allow yourself to spend some time there whilst starting to develop your skills and network. As the months go by, you'll slowly start to become extremely efficient in your role so you can then start fighting for promotions. As you start to grow your career within the same company structure, you'll onboard more responsibilities and challenges that will help you grow even faster if you succeed. At this point, you should be able to absorb all protocols, techniques, knowledge, and networks possible to obtain. At a certain point in time, if you learn and absorb 99% of everything in one or two years, even if you stay another five, you will only absorb an extra 1%, so the ROI is far too small for the time you'd be exchanging. When you hit this learning wall and feel as if you could do your job with a blindfold on, it's once again time to move on to a more established, higher-tier company. At this point in your career, you should have enough experience, network, knowledge, and perceived value to be attractive to tier 1 companies.

Third Job: 2 Years+

Third time's the charm is what they say, and just like Goldilocks with the three bears, this one should be just right. On your third job, you should be aiming for nothing less than a tier 1 company. This is the moment when your career will really start to take off and your network will become exceptional, alongside your paycheck, of course. At this time, you should be earning a much higher salary and spending the most of your time engaging with among the most established individuals, projects, and companies in the industry. In this position, you will soon realize that people you've never heard of before start reaching out to you and asking for advice or help. Very quickly, you will find that you're on the other side of the bridge, where the remaining 99% of the industry is trying to get to. By staying humble, kind, and genuine, you can really transform yourself into a prominent figure and start to enjoy the fruits of your labor. It's also important to note that you should try to keep a position in a tier 1 company for at least two years if you wish to remain an employee in the space and not an independent. If you leave after a few months and try to join a different tier 1 company, they will find it very odd that you left your prior position very fast, and this can sprout doubt on your work efficiency, hence making hiring you hard. If, however, you're able to stay within that tier 1 company for at least two years and maybe get a promotion or two during that time, virtually any tier 1 company in this space will hire you as you have a stellar track record.

As you evolve in the world of Web3, you'll find yourself naturally adding and modifying your initial roadmap as you go along. Keeping in mind these timelines will help you structure a very advantageous profile that will open many doors for you in and outside of this space. As an example, some extremely well-established individuals can go on to advise large, tier 1 projects, CEXs, accelerators, among other Web3 companies, but they can also go on to advise governments, hedge funds, traditional finance companies, banks, and more. Although the industry is evolving at the speed of light while being forced under other-worldly pressure from regulators and government policies, there will always be work. No matter how they try to stop the Web3 expansion, it will always bounce back immediately after taking a different shape or form to absorb that blow. As we advance, we're more than likely to see one of the newest, biggest, and most fruitful sectors to work in, even more so than today, as blockchain technology will become completely mainstream one day or another. For this reason, working in Web3 is one of the most promising and exciting sectors of work that anyone with ambition could hope to work in.

Final Thoughts

If you do decide to make the change and start a career in crypto, I sincerely wish you the best of luck and hope that it will bring as much passion, joy, fun, and financial freedom as it has done for myself and so many others in this space. Finally, may this book guide you along the way by ensuring that you're always one step ahead and ready to work in the sensational world of crypto!

Glossary

1) Crypto – Cryptography is the practice of creating and understanding codes that keep information secret.

2) Web3 – Web 3.0 is the coming generation of the Internet. Web 3.0 Definition | CoinMarketCap

3) Cryptocurrency – A digital currency produced by a public network, rather than any government, that uses cryptography to make sure payments are sent and received safely.

4) Market Maker – A person or company that continuously buys and sells shares in particular companies for particular prices.

5) Blockchain – A system used to make a digital record of all the occasions a cryptocurrency (= a digital currency such as bitcoin) is bought or sold, and that is constantly growing as more blocks are added.

6) Altcoin – Any cryptocurrency (= a digital currency that is produced by a public network rather than by a government and uses special codes to keep it secure) that is not bitcoin (= the first cryptocurrency to be established).

© Alexander Rees-Evans 2024
A. Rees-Evans, *So You Want to Work in Crypto*,
https://doi.org/10.1007/979-8-8688-0503-5

7) KYC – Know Your Client (KYC) is a standard in the investment industry that ensures advisors can verify a client's identity and know their client's investment knowledge and financial profile. Know Your Client (KYC): What It Means and Compliance Requirements (investopedia.com)

8) Exchange – An online trading platform that is used to buy, sell, and exchange cryptocurrencies. Exchanges convert fiat currency (dollars, euros, etc.) to crypto (Bitcoin, Ethereum, etc.), and vice versa. Definition of crypto exchange | PCMag

9) Degen – Shorthand for Degenerate. Degen trading or Degen mode is when a trader does trading without due diligence and research, aping into signals and FOMO into pumps. A Degen Trader does not know about metrics like FDV or TVL, nor do they care. They will buy because the asset logo looks cute, or because the slogan is memeable, or because some twit-famous anime girl on the Internet says she's looking into crypto, and the first two shill comments get more likes than others. Essentially, a degen trader buys into an asset not because they see value; rather, they do so with the belief that others will join in after them and speculate on the price swings. Definition of Degen | CoinGecko

10) CEX – Centralized exchanges (CEXs) are a type of cryptocurrency exchange that is operated by a company that owns it in a centralized manner. Centralized Exchange (CEX) Definition | CoinMarketCap.

11) KOL – A key opinion leader (KOL) is an influential person with in-depth knowledge about a specific topic. They have commanded respect and recognition for their expertise and views and can influence their audience's behavior through exceptional communication skills. Collabstr | What is a KOL in Marketing? Key Opinion Leaders Explained.

12) IDO – An initial dex offering (IDX) is an alternative to an initial coin offering (ICO). Initial Dex Offering (IDO) Definition | CoinMarketCap.

13) SAFT – A Simple Agreement for Future Token (SAFT) is a contractual agreement at the time of launch of a token, creating ownership rights for token investors at a future date. Simple Agreement for Future Token (SAFT) Definition | CoinMarketCap.

14) Unique Selling Proposition – A unique selling proposition (USP) is a short statement of what differentiates a brand from competitors: a product benefit, feature, or company trait that consumers value and will come to know the company for. It's also called a unique selling point. What is a Unique Selling Proposition? (2024 Examples) (makingthatsale.com)

15) TVL – Total value locked (TVL) is the overall value of crypto assets deposited in a decentralized finance (DeFi) protocol – or in DeFi protocols generally. It has emerged as a key metric for gauging interest in that particular sector of the crypto industry. Why TVL Matters in DeFi: Total Value Locked Explained (coindesk.com)

16) DApp – A decentralized application (dapp) is an application built on a decentralized network that combines a smart contract and a frontend user interface. On Ethereum, smart contracts are accessible and transparent – like open APIs – so your dapp can even include a smart contract that someone else has written. Introduction to dapps | ethereum.org

17) Gas Fees – "Gas fees" are the transaction fees that users pay to miners on a blockchain protocol to have their transaction included in the block. What Are Gas Fees? | CoinMarketCap

18) Block Time – Block time measures the time it takes the miners or validators within a network to verify transactions within one block and produce a new block in that blockchain. What Is Block Time? What It Measures, Verification, and Example (investopedia.com)

19) POS – Proof of Stake is a popular alternative consensus mechanism to Proof of Work. Instead of needing computing power to validate transactions, validators must stake coins. This fact drastically reduces the energy consumption needed. Proof of Stake can also improve decentralization, security, and scalability. What Is Proof of Stake (PoS)? | Binance Academy

20) DAO – A decentralized autonomous organization (DAO) is founded upon and governed by a set of computer-defined rules and blockchain-based smart contracts. Decentralized Autonomous Organizations (DAO) Definition | CoinMarketCap

21) Proof-of-History, or PoH – A novel technique used in blockchain systems to ensure that historical data is accurate and hasn't been (and cannot be) tampered with. How Does Proof-of-History (PoH) Work? | CoinMarketCap

22) EVM – The EVM is the program that executes its application code, or smart contracts, as they are called, providing a run-time environment for them that runs on top of the Ethereum network. What's more, the EVM is Turing-complete and can thus run any program coded in any programming language, thereby allowing developers to easily create custom smart contracts and DApps for the burgeoning Web3 space. What is an Ethereum Virtual Machine (EVM) and how does it work? (cointelegraph.com)

23) AnyTrust Guarantee – AnyTrust relies instead on an external Data Availability Committee (hereafter, "the Committee") to store data and provide it on demand. The Committee has N members, of which AnyTrust assumes at least two are honest. This means that if N – 1 Committee members promise to provide access to some data, at least one of the promising parties must be honest. Since there are two honest members and only one failed to make the promise, it follows that at least one of the promisers must be honest — and that honest member will provide data when it is needed to ensure the chain can properly function. Inside AnyTrust | Arbitrum Docs

24) Initial Exchange Offering – An IEO, or *Initial Exchange Offering*, is a fundraising exercise through a pre-sale of tokens on an exchange platform. The term is directly modeled on the term *Initial Coin Offering* (ICO), itself modelled on *Initial Public Offering* (IPO). https://cryptoast.fr/ieo-explications-definition/

25) Avalanche Consensus – The avalanche consensus relies on the principle of Repeated Sub-Sampling Voting. https://medium.com/coinmonks/avalanche-fundamentals-consensus-mechanism-explained-cb2db0a59fb8

26) Gwei – The term gwei refers to a small denomination of ether (ETH), which is the native currency of the Ethereum blockchain. Specifically, a unit of gwei is defined as one-billionth (one Nano) of an ether. So 1 gwei equals 0.000000001 or 10e-9 ETH. Conversely, 1 ETH equals one billion (10e9) gwei. https://academy.binance.com/en/glossary/gwei

27) Fork – Cryptocurrencies like Bitcoin and Ethereum are powered by decentralized, open-source software called a blockchain. A fork happens whenever a community makes a change to the blockchain's protocol, or basic set of rules. https://www.coinbase.com/en-fr/learn/crypto-basics/what-is-a-fork

28) Node – In crypto, however, a node is one of the components that run a blockchain's algorithm to verify and authenticate each transaction. https://fr-fr.worldcoin.org/articles/what-is-a-blockchain-node

29) ICO – An Initial coin offering is a crypto fundraise in which a crypto asset is created and offered to public investors. https://www.delubac.com/en/glossary/crypto/ico/

30) Oracle – Blockchain oracles are entities that connect blockchains to external systems, thereby enabling smart contracts to execute based upon inputs and outputs from the real world. https://chain.link/education/blockchain-oracles

31) TPS – Transactions Per Second (TPS) is the number of transactions that a network can process in a second. It is a measurement used to evaluate the transaction speed of a network. https://www.ledger.com/academy/glossary/transactions-per-second-tps

32) DAG – A directed acyclic graph (DAG) is a type of data structure aiming to improve upon the shortcomings of a conventional blockchain. One difference between a DAG and a standard blockchain is that DAGs have no blocks, though transactions come through via nodes. https://crypto.com/glossary/fr/directed-acyclic-graph-dag

33) Staking – Staking cryptocurrency means locking up coins to maintain the security of a blockchain network and earning rewards in return. https://academy.binance.com/en/articles/what-is-staking

34) Vesting – The process of locking down cryptocurrency tokens or coins for a predetermined amount of time before allowing the token holder to fully access or transfer them is known as crypto vesting. `https://cointelegraph.com/explained/vesting-in-crypto-explained`

35) Sniper Bot – A sniper bot is an automated instrument that is developed to make transactions quickly in response to predetermined market conditions. The key features of sniper bots in the cryptocurrency sphere include precision in trade execution, which is determined by predetermined parameters to ensure favorable market entrance and exit positions. `https://cointelegraph.com/explained/what-are-sniper-bots-and-how-to-stop-token-sniping-exploits`

36) MEV Bot/Frontrunner – Front running happens when a market participant is able to use information on pending transactions to place their own ahead of another's buy or sell order.

   `https://keyrock.com/understand-front-running-crypto-markets/`

37) Cliff – A cliff is a period where no tokens are awarded. This, in turn, delays the start of the crypto vesting schedule. `https://phemex.com/blogs/crypto-vesting-and-cliffs`

38) Digital Nomad – Digital nomads are people who are location-independent and use technology to perform their job, living a nomadic lifestyle. Digital nomads work remotely, telecommuting

rather than being physically present at a company's headquarters or office. The digital nomad lifestyle has been made possible through several innovations, including content management software, cheap Internet access through WiFi, smartphones, and Voice-over-Internet Protocol (VoIP) to contact clients and employers. In addition, the growth of a gig economy has played a role, too. `https://www.investopedia.com/terms/d/digital-nomad.asp`

39) Fear and Greed Index – The Fear & Greed Index is a measure developed by CNN Business to gauge investor sentiment. It indicates how emotions influence the amount investors are willing to pay for stocks, which in turn provides a window into whether stocks are fairly priced at any given point in time. The Fear & Greed Index: What It Is and How It Works (investopedia.com)

40) Cap Table – A capitalization table is a spreadsheet or table that shows the equity capitalization of a company. It's also known as a cap table and is most commonly used for startups and early stage businesses, but all types of companies can use it as well. The capitalization table is generally an intricate breakdown of a company's shareholders' equity. Capitalization (Cap) Table: What It Is and How to Create and Maintain One (investopedia.com)

41) Nodes – A crypto node is a computer that is part of a blockchain network. It maintains the latest record of transactions and ensures that all participants adhere to the network's rules. Nodes are components of a blockchain network, facilitating decentralized transactions. They aim to validate and process transactions without the need for a centralized entity, striving to ensure the integrity and security of the network. What is a node in cryptocurrency? | Coinbase

42) KOL – KOL stands for Key Opinion Leader. These individuals hold significant influence within a specific industry or community and are recognized for their expertise and credibility. In the context of crypto marketing, KOLs play a pivotal role in shaping opinions, driving engagement, and influencing purchasing decisions. coinideology.com

43) Non-Disclosure Agreement – A non-disclosure agreement (NDA) is a legally binding contract that establishes a confidential relationship between two parties: one that holds sensitive information and the other that will receive that sensitive information. The latter agrees that the information they receive won't be made available to others. An NDA may also be referred to as a confidentiality agreement. Non-Disclosure Agreement (NDA) Explained, With Pros and Cons (investopedia.com)

Index

© Alexander Rees-Evans 2024
A. Rees-Evans, *So You Want to Work in Crypto*,
https://doi.org/10.1007/979-8-8688-0503-5

Y, Z